Heresies

THOMAS SZASZ is Professor of Psychiatry at the State University of New York Upstate Medical Center in Syracuse, New York. He is a member of the editorial board of *The Humanist, Journal of Humanistic Psychology, Journal of Drug Addiction,* and *Contemporary Psychoanalysis,* and of the board of consultants of *The Psychoanalytic Review;* a member of the American Psychoanalytic Association; a fellow of American Psychiatric Association; and a co-founder of the American Association for the Abolition of Involuntary Mental Hospitalization. He is the author of more than two hundred articles and book reviews and of numerous books.

Other Books by Thomas Szasz

PAIN AND PLEASURE

THE MYTH OF MENTAL ILLNESS

LAW, LIBERTY, AND PSYCHIATRY

IDEOLOGY AND INSANITY

THE MANUFACTURE OF MADNESS

PSYCHIATRIC JUSTICE

THE AGE OF MADNESS (ed.)

THE SECOND SIN

THE ETHICS OF PSYCHOANALYSIS

CEREMONIAL CHEMISTRY

Heresies

THOMAS SZASZ

ANCHOR BOOKS
ANCHOR PRESS/DOUBLEDAY
GARDEN CITY, NEW YORK
1976

Anchor Books Edition: 1976
Copyright © 1976 by Thomas S. Szasz
All rights reserved
Printed in the United States of America
First Edition

Library of Congress Cataloging in Publication Data

Szasz, Thomas Stephen, 1920–
Heresies.

Includes bibliographical references.
1. Psychiatry—Quotations, maxims, etc.
2. Psychology—Quotations, maxims, etc.   I.   Title.
RC461.S89   616.8′9
ISBN: 0-385-11162-2
Library of Congress Catalog Card Number 75-30131

"The word heresy is derived from the Greek *hairesis* which originally meant an act of choosing, and so came to signify a set of philosophical opinions or the school professing to them. As so used the term was neutral, but once appropriated by Christianity it began to convey a note of disapproval. This was because the church from the start regarded itself as the custodian of a divinely imparted revelation, which it alone was authorized to expound . . . Thus any interpretation which differed from the official one was necessarily 'heretical' in the new, pejorative sense."

"Heresy," Encyclopaedia Britannica (1973)

Acknowledgments

I wish to thank Ronald Carino, Joseph DeVeaugh-Geiss, Jonathan Ecker, Kathleen McNamara, Lynn Haun Wilcox, and George, Margot, and Susan Szasz, my friends and family, for many useful suggestions; Elizabeth Knappman, my editor, for giving this book its final shape and for her unfailing helpfulness; Georgie Remer, for exceptionally conscientious and competent copy-editing of the manuscript; and Debbie Murphy, my secretary, for her devoted labors.

Contents

Preface

This is a collection of observations and reflections on a variety of subjects, but mainly on language and law, and on medicine, morals, and madness. It is thus a continuation and extension of several of my previous books, and especially of *The Second Sin*. While it may be more rewarding for those who are familiar with some of my earlier writings, it may be more refreshing for those who are not. In any event, to understand it, and I hope to enjoy it, requires no special competence or knowledge, but only a willingness to think for oneself.

unconscious?"—as if not believing in the unconscious were like not believing in the liver—it is because my disbelief offends his belief. A hematologist or Hebraist couldn't care less about whether or not I believe in the unconscious, but he might be quite interested in whether or not I believe in the genetic causation of leukemia or the divinity of Jesus. And so it goes. The point is that what is heretical for one person may be heroic for another and irrelevant for a third.

Most of the heresies in this book are of the same type as those mentioned above about religion and psychoanalysis. That is, they pertain to matters where language is used in two ways, literally and metaphorically; where the true believer speaks metaphorically but claims that he asserts literal truths; and where heresy may consist of no more than insisting that a metaphoric truth may be a literal falsehood. One's wife may be a witch; but she cannot be a "real" witch. However, there are people who believe that their wives are witches and act accordingly, murderously, toward them. Psychiatrists say that such a person is psychotic and act toward him as if they believed that he was a "real" patient. So are metaphors created and literalized, confirmed as "real" and unmasked as "myth," new ones formed, literalized, and so forth—in the cycles of what we call individual, organizational, and cultural lives and deaths. This is what poets and politicians, psychotics and psychiatrists, therapists and theologians have in common: they all deal with metaphors that sustain the dignity and lives of some and destroy those of others; and they all deal with metaphors mendaciously, insisting that metaphorical meaning is literal and that literal meaning is metaphorical. The result of all this is the mystification, the nonsense, and the outright prevarication that make up a large part of the semantic air people in all cultures have always exhaled and then, mistaking it for the pure air of the mountains or oceans, have enthusiastically rebreathed.

Still, just as when the concentration of carbon dioxide in the air exceeds a certain limit and interferes with breathing, so there comes a point when belief in the reality of literalized metaphor exceeds a certain limit and interferes with knowing. When that happens, whole groups and civilizations lose, as it were, their sense of humor: they actually come to believe, for example, that certain moral injunctions were given to their forefathers because they were God's favorite children; that a piece of bread is the body of a god; that pregnancy is a disease which justifies abortion as a treatment and requires that delivery take place in a hospital superintended by doctors; or that the unconscious is a part of a mental apparatus just as real as the liver or kidneys and hence requiring a science of its own. I could go on, but as that is what I do in this book there is no need to do so here. Instead, I shall do something I do not do in the book: namely, show, as a warning about where the literalization of our favorite metaphors may lead us, where the literalization of one of the favorite metaphors of Christianity has led our ancestors.

II

The literalization of the metaphor of the Last Supper creates the image that Jesus is alive. If so, He can be killed again. Incredible as it may sound to the contemporary reader, this belief was actually held in Europe until relatively recent times. For about three hundred years, from the thirteenth until the sixteenth centuries, there were repeated episodes of Jews being accused of stabbing the sacramental wafer and making it bleed—justifying the killing of thousands of Jews. Moreover, the colloquial characterization of Jews as "Christ-killers," even in modern anti-Semitism, also points to the power that literalized metaphors exercise over the human mind: for this epithet must be read as casting blame for the death of Jesus not only on some Jews who lived a long time ago, but also on Jews who are the speaker's contemporaries.

The story of the "bleeding" Eucharist is a fascinating, but astonishingly neglected, chapter of medieval history. The following is, of course, but a bird's eye view of it.

According to Eugene Gaughran,[1] the first authentic reference to mysterious blood appearing on bread is the report of classical historians concerning the siege of Tyre, in what is now Lebanon, in 332 B.C. Diodorus Siculus, the Greek historian, gave this account of the phenomenon: "At the distribution of the rations on the Macedonian side, the broken pieces of bread had a bloody look."[2]

The exact cause of this reddish coloration, which was often mistaken for blood, was not discovered until 1823, when the Italian naturalist Bartolomeo Bizio identified, named, and described the saprophytic bacterium *Serratia marcescens* as its cause. This widely distributed bacterium, which grows readily in starchy foods, produces a blood-red pigment. To those who believed that the Host was the body of Christ and not just a piece of bread, the occurrence of this pigment in the bread thus had momentous significance.

One of the earliest reports of such bacterial discoloration of the sacramental wafer was reported in 1247. In the village of Beelitz, in Germany, "A maid held the Host in her mouth during communion. Later she sold it to Jews who stabbed it, kept the blood which flowed from it, and gave the Host back to her. The Miraculous blood made the Church of Beelitz famous."[3] There is no mention of any harm coming to the Jews in this case.

Soon, however, stories of "bloody" Hosts become the backdrops for their mass murder.

Gaughran reports a typical incident of this sort:

In Paris on Easter [1290] a woman is said to have taken the Host from her mouth after communion and given it to a Jew to redeem a pawned dress. The Jew boiled the Host in water without destroying it. He then stabbed it and the water became complete red. The Host flew by itself onto the table where Christians saw it. The Jew confessed the deed and was burned.[4]

Here are several more such accounts:

1298 A.D., Nuremburg, Germany

The Jews are said to have stolen the Holy Host of the Christians, scorned it, and beat it in a mortar and pestle, and blood came out of it. The Jews in Nuremburg were destroyed by fire and sword, and the persecution extended into eastern France.

❊ ❊ ❊

1299 A.D., Röttingen, France

The Jews of Röttingen were reported to have bought Hosts at Easter time in order to draw blood from them. They stabbed them and powdered them in a mortar. Many Jews are said to have been killed by the Christians.

❊ ❊ ❊

1399 A.D., Poznan, Poland

A girl sold a Host to the Jews who stabbed it until blood appeared. They threw it into a swamp. A shepherd saw the Host flying about and the oxen knelt in adoration. The girl was burned with the Jews.

❊ ❊ ❊

1492 A.D., Sternberg, Germany

In the state of Mecklenburg an unscrupulous priest, Peter Dane, in order to redeem pawned goods, gave two Hosts to a Jew, Eleazar. He had sanctified them on July 10. On the Friday before the Feast of St. James, July 20, the Jews defiled the Hosts and stabbed them until blood flowed and stained the table through three layers of cloth. The wounded Hosts flew about on the table top. The Jews were frightened and wished to return the Hosts. Eleazar's wife returned to Peter Dane the bloody Hosts concealed in the socket of a candle stick holder, the whole wrapped in a cloth. He denounced them because his conscience bothered him. All the Jews who knew about this were put on trial and more than twenty of them were burned on Simon Judas Day on a hill near Sternberg, which since has been called Judenberg. Judenberg is a place where the legislative assembly of Mecklenburg for many years held its open air sessions.[5]

And so it went. I cite these episodes concerning the stabbing and bleeding of the Host to show where the literalization of the central metaphor of Christianity—of sacramental wafer as the body of the Son of God—could lead. It actually led to the interpretation of a reddish pigment in starchy material as blood, as the blood being the blood of Jesus, and as the cause of the shedding of His blood being the Jews. This line of reasoning—which we now recognize as transparently literalized and strategic—justified the "rightful" killing of Jews as murderers. The same reddish discoloration of starchy foods had, of course, been observed by other people at other times, none of whom gave it this particular interpretation. One is reminded here of sayings such as "One sees what one is prepared to see" and "Opportunity favors the prepared mind." When men are prepared to see the Jews as Christ-killers, and when they want to kill the Jews for killing the Son of God, they will then perceive the reddish discoloration of the sacramental wafer as blood. And their "religious" interpretation of its red color will not seem inconsistent to them with the fact that the same discoloration also occurs in bread that has not been consecrated—in other words, in bread (literal bread, for eating), as well as in Bread (metaphorical bread, for worshiping by Christians and for "killing" by Jews).

III

The contemporary reader may be tempted to dismiss all this as the magical thinking of medieval peasants. That would be a mistake. For if mistaking the bacterial discoloration of bread for the bleeding body of Jesus seems bizarre to the contemporary, intellectually enlightened reader, what does the belief in "ritual murder" seem like to him? By "ritual murder" I refer to the belief of some Christians, still current during my childhood in Hungary, that in order to celebrate the Passover holidays properly, the Jews need the blood of a Christian child as an ingredient for making the unleavened bread, or matzoh. To obtain such blood, so this accusation of ritual murder goes, the Jews kill Christian children before the Passover. Curiously, this idea seems to have sprung up at about the same time as did the organized belief in witchcraft—that is, in the twelfth century. In 1144, a young English boy, William of Norwich, was said to have been killed for such a purpose. Revealingly, he was supposed to have been killed by crucifixion.[6]

Although there was no evidence for this particular charge, the belief quickly spread and marked the beginning of a long series of anti-Semitic persecutions throughout Europe. Even in the nineteenth century, there were forty-two recorded cases of charges of ritual murder being brought against Jews, one of the most famous being that which took place at Tiszaeszlar, a village in southern Hungary. On April 1, 1882, a fourteen-year-old Calvinist girl disappeared near the home of

Joseph Scharf, the sexton of the Jewish synagogue in the village. Her mother accused Scharf of having murdered the girl in order to get Christian blood for matzoh. A local magistrate forced Scharf's son to confess participation in the crime. At the trial, Scharf was exonerated and the conspiracy to convict him was exposed. Because of the enormous publicity which this trial generated, it became Europe's best known case of the judicial persecution of Jews prior to the Dreyfus affair in France.[7]

Another famous case occurred in 1899 at Polna, Bohemia, where Leopold Hilsner, a shoemaker's apprentice, was accused of having murdered a nineteen-year-old seamstress. The prosecutor injected the motive of ritual murder into his charge. What gives this case special poignancy is that after a local court had sentenced Hilsner to death, Thomas Masaryk—who was later to go on to be the founding father and first President of Czechoslovakia—published several brochures and articles pleading for a new trial. In the second trial, where there was no reference to ritual murder, Hilsner was sentenced to life imprisonment. In his book on Austrian intellectual history, William Johnston, in an effort to recreate the temper of those times, concludes this story with the following important observation:

> Coinciding with the climax of the Dreyfus affair, the Polna case intimidated Jews throughout Austria. One university professor, himself a converted Jew, appalled Masaryk by conceding, "You know that I am a Jew myself and I am convinced that this ritual murder business is merely superstition. But this case proves the possible existence of a secret sect which might after all practice ritual murder."[8]

This Jewish attitude, at once pathetic and shocking, became widespread during the Dreyfus affair and proved literally fatal when the Nazis rose to power. It

has its root, in my opinion, in the recognition of the ir-
reconcilable tensions between Christians and Jews. Judaism is anti-Christian and Christianity is anti-Jewish in a
way that neither is, say, anti-Buddhist or anti-Shintoist.
This is, quite simply, because Christianity is a Jewish
heresy and because the image of the Jew as Christ-killer
became, historically, an integral part of Christianity itself. This, I submit, accounts for the fact that "although
many Christian writers and theologians, including a
dozen popes, beginning with Gregory X in the thirteenth
century, have refuted the ritual murder charge against
the Jews, . . . it appears to be impossible to stamp out
this libelous canard."[9]

But the Christian belief in Jewish ritual murder is no
"canard." It is rather the tragic consequence of the literalization of one of its leading metaphors, namely, of
its deity having been murdered by the Jews, dying,
being resurrected—and then being murdered over and
over again. To admit that all this is, after all, only a
mythic story, that the God, Jesus, is only a metaphor—
that is easier said than done. For, as Barrows Dunham in
his brilliant history of heresy so clearly shows, literalized
metaphors are the life blood of organizations. Hence,
they cannot afford such metaphors to be recognized as
such:

> . . . the future explorers of space will find no divinities;
> and, though a thing not found in one place may yet exist
> somewhere else, the always disappointed search is bound
> to tire. In the end, all that will have happened doctrinally
> is that a metaphor has been discovered to be a metaphor,
> but one cannot expect that organizations whose unity de-
> pends on taking metaphor literally will be pleased with the
> revelation.[10]

IV

Organizations are indeed not pleased when what they claim are literal truths, others consider to be literalized metaphors. The Roman Catholic Church's displeasure at such an interpretation of the Eucharist was formally articulated by the Council of Trent in 1552 in a decree still not formally rescinded. It declares:

> If any one shall say that, in the Holy Sacrament of the Eucharist there remains, together with the Body and Blood of our Lord Jesus Christ, the substance of the Bread and Wine, and shall deny that wonderful and singular conversion of the whole substances of the Bread into [His] Body and the Wine into [His] Blood, the species only of the Bread and Wine remaining—which conversion the Catholic Church most fittingly calls Transubstantiation—let him be anathema.[11]

The point to remember, however, is that so long as there is tension between the individual and the group of which he is a member, there will be heresy, whatever it might be called. The individual must think for himself. More than anything else, that is what makes him an individual. The group, on the other hand, must want its members to echo its beliefs. A group completely indifferent to the beliefs of its members would not long remain a group.

It follows, then, that although the structure of heresy may be regarded as constant, its content will depend on the dominant beliefs of the group in which it arises. When peoples and societies are held together, as many had been until the Enlightenment, by the ideals and images of Christianity, then heresy is deviation from the official beliefs and dogmas of the clergy. And when peoples and societies are held together, as many now are, by the ideals and images of science and technology, medicine and health, then heresy is deviation from the official beliefs and dogmas of scientists and doctors.

Thus, today, one of our leading literalized metaphors is our image of the state as a wise and just father whose ministrations will provide "social justice" and "welfare" for all. Another is our image of disease and death as enemies invading our otherwise healthy bodies, whose attacks can be successfully repulsed if we help our doctors develop a "therapeutic armamentarium" powerful enough for the task. A third is our image of disagreement and discord as mental disorder due to a medical disease and hence eradicable like malaria. It is these metaphors, and some others, and the consequences of their literalizations—which are every bit as odd and awful as were the consequences of the literalizations of the metaphors of Christianity—that are the main targets of my heresies.

Introduction

REFERENCES

1. See E. R. L. Gaughran, "From Superstition to Science: The History of a Bacterium," *Transactions of the New York Academy of Sciences*, Series II, 30: 3–24 (Jan.), 1969. My review of the accounts of the "bleeding Host" is based entirely on Gaughran's excellent essay.
2. Ibid., p. 3.
3. Ibid., p. 7.
4. Ibid., p. 9.
5. Ibid., pp. 9–12.
6. See "Human sacrifice," in the Encyclopaedia Britannica (1973), vol. 11, p. 830.
7. W. M. Johnston, *The Austrian Mind: An Intellectual and Social History, 1848–1938* (Berkeley: University of California Press, 1972), p. 344.
8. Ibid., p. 28.
9. "Human sacrifice," Encyclopaedia Britannica, vol. 11, p. 830.
10. B. Dunham, *Heroes and Heretics: A Political History of Western Thought* (New York: A. A. Knopf, 1964), p. 315.
11. See "Transubstantiation," Encyclopaedia Britannica (1949), vol. 22, p. 417. Although some Catholic theologians have tried to restate this doctrine in terms of "transsignification" and "transfinalization," in his encyclical *Mysterium Fidei* (September 3, 1965), Pope Paul VI "called for a retention of the full reality of the Catholic faith about the Presence of Christ in the Eucharist, and specifically for a retention of the dogma of transubstantiation, together with the received terminology in which it has been expressed, particularly at the Council of Trent" ("Transubstantiation," Encyclopaedia Britannica (1973), vol. 22, p. 175).

Family

There are two kinds of parental love, each diametrically opposed to the other. One expresses itself in the gentle but firm expectation that the child "can do it"; the other, in the vague and vacuous declaration of support for whatever the child "wants to do." Implicit in the former, which encourages competence, is the parent's respect for the child; implicit in the latter, which discourages competence, is the parent's disrespect for him or her.

* * *

The so-called permissive parent raises his children believing that if only he "gives" them enough, they will become "giving" persons. He is then surprised that when his children reach adulthood they know only how to "take." Would he also be surprised if he taught his children only to catch balls, and they did not become great pitchers?

* * *

Prolonged, unrelieved association between children and parents, husbands and wives, is likely to prove unbearably irritating to one or both parties. Out of this elementary fact are fashioned elaborate psychiatric theories about why and how parents drive their children crazy and marital partners drive each other crazy. Actually, although people need a certain amount of human contact, both physical and spiritual, too much contact, especially between unequals, is painful and stimulates intense feelings of antagonism toward those who infringe on one's life-space. This is why most close human relationships are so often unsatisfactory: for example, children often experience parental protection as deprivation of independence, and husbands and wives often experience intimacy as deprivation of privacy.

*   *   *

Because children cannot accomplish as much as adults, they are usually rewarded for effort. But as soon as possible, they should be taught that what counts in life is not effort but achievement. Children overrewarded for effort often continue to seek approval for their effort instead of for their achievement. This dooms them to failure: for if they succeed, they succeed only at trying hard; and if they fail, they fail dismally.

*   *   *

Although it is hard for a son to compete with a very successful father, it is even harder for him to compete with a very unsuccessful one. This is because most young men find the prospect of their own relative failure easier to bear than the prospect of being the instruments of their father's humiliation.

Marriage

Marriages are said to be made in heaven, which must be why they don't work here on earth.

* * *

Young love rests largely on loneliness and lust. This is why it is so poor a basis for marriage, which must rest largely on affection and respect.

* * *

Marriage: tenured togetherness.

* * *

Every marriage is an "arrangement." Hence, we should distinguish not between marriages and arrangements, but among different types of arrangements—marital and nonmarital.

* * *

Trial marriage is to real marriage as buying and selling stocks on paper are to buying and selling them on the stock market.

* * *

Husband and wife are not so much sexual partners as they are identity accretions, each being defined by the other. This is why the husband's or wife's beauty or ugliness, health or sickness, wealth or poverty, behavior or misbehavior, high or low social rank—making each a source of pride or shame for the other—have far more to do with the stability or instability of the marital relationship than does the quality of the sexual relationship between them.

* * *

By becoming "one body" in marriage, wives can injure their husbands by eating too much and husbands can injure their wives by drinking too much. What psychiatrists have long called, and what the public now accepts as, "self-destructive" behavior is thus often the exact opposite: an attempt to preserve oneself by destroying what one regards as one's "parasite."

* * *

A metaphor for many a modern marriage: two competent swimmers in the water, safe but solitary; they decide to play, one pretending to drown, the other pretending to rescue; grappling in this charade, they sink, panic, and drown together.

* * *

Men are married to their work and are identified by what they do. Women are married to their husbands and are identified by who their mates are. The wonder is not that contemporary marriages work so poorly, but that they work at all.

* * *

Men lose their names when they go to prison; women, when they get married.

* * *

Since many young women are enslaved—to their parents as children, and to males as females—they often marry to escape from slavery. Once married, they often behave as both slaves and rebels, that is, as rebellious slaves. Zelda Fitzgerald and Sylvia Plath seem to have experienced and enacted this predicament. The options in life for such women are few, and all but one of them are tragic.

One option for such a woman is to put up a feeble struggle against her husband, convince herself of the hopelessness of the odds against her, and allow herself to be crushed. The result is chronic invalidism, mental illness with periodic or permanent institutionalization, or some other "living death."

Another option is to put up a fierce struggle and crush her husband. The result is the life of a martyr, "putting up" with an incompetent, alcoholic, or otherwise debased husband.

Still another option is to set herself free of her husband and, unable to cope with freedom, succumb to misfortune, illness, or suicide.

Finally, there is the option for her to set herself free and to become an independent, separate, and whole person.

*   *   *

Traditional or arranged marriage was a fine institution for legitimizing men and women as adults and for raising children; it could be ruined, and was ruined, by one thing only: the expectation that the partners, in addition to these obligations, should also love each other and enjoy each other as sexual partners.

Modern or romantic marriage is also a fine institution for legitimizing men and women as adults and for friendship and sex; it can be ruined, and is ruined, by one thing only: the expectation that the partners, in addition to these obligations, should also be financially re-

Love

The many faces of love: the child loves out of dependency; the lover, out of desire; the newlywed, out of duty; the spouse and the parent, out of devotion; the long-married and the grandparent, out of dedication; and the aged and dying, out of desperation.

* * *

Infants love the persons who feed them. And we consider it a sign of maturity when children learn to love the food that relieves their hunger rather than the person who cooks or serves it.

In adults we reverse these judgments. Men and women are expected to love those who satisfy their sexual hunger. And we consider it a sign of immaturity if they love not their sexual partners but only their partners' erotic attributes.

* * *

To the dominant person, love is lust; to the submissive, it is protection. This is why rich and important persons, whether men or women, often have poor and unimportant "lovers"; and why poor and unimportant persons often have rich and important "loves." The former arrangement satisfies the lust of those who have "lovers"; the latter satisfies the need for protection of those who have "loves."

*   *   *

When men and women are "in love," they share the mistaken belief that they live in the same world; when they "love" one another, they acknowledge that they live in different worlds, but are prepared once in a while to cross the chasm between them.

Sex

Fellatio: oral contraception.

*   *   *

Promiscuity: the envious and frustrated person's name for pluralism and variety in sexual relations.

*   *   *

Masturbation: taking things into one's own hands; which is why authorities either prohibit or prescribe it, making certain, in one way or another, of maintaining control over the individual.

*   *   *

Sex therapists: pimps and procurers with clinical credentials.

*   *   *

Pornography is to sex as vulgarity is to language.

*   *   *

The difference between erotic art and pornography is roughly the same as the difference between sexual desire and genital itching.

*   *   *

There are two sexes. One could be called "complementary" to the other. But in fact one is called the "opposite" of the other. Is this not more revealing of the true relations between the sexes than the whole lexicon of love?

* * *

Sexual desire is to copulation as appetite is to eating. Each may be stimulated or inhibited by the appearance and fragrance of the object of its craving. Women who groom and act as if they wanted to arouse every man's sexual interest in them do indeed make sexual "objects" of themselves, as the feminists claim. By the same token, women who groom and act as if they wanted to inhibit every man's sexual interest in them, make nonsexual "objects" of themselves.

* * *

Sexual attraction and love between equals is the exception rather than the rule. Men are enamored of women "above" or "beneath" them, and vice versa. Lady Chatterley's lover was a gamekeeper, not a lord.

* * *

Pleasure in genital eroticism is literal sexuality. Pleasure in eating, defecating, urinating, and so forth is metaphorical sexuality. In his theories of sexuality, Freud first metaphorized human pleasures and then literalized his own metaphors, insisting that nonsexual pleasures are not merely *like* sexual pleasures, but *are* sexual pleasures.

* * *

Orgasm is the quintessential paradox, and perhaps because of it, the quintessential pleasure in the entire range of human experience. This is because orgasm is the controlled experience of loss of control. If the loss of control over sexual arousal and response is overcontrolled or if the control under which the loss is experienced is inadequate, the orgastic experience is impaired or absent. Conversely, the more unrestrained is the loss of control and the more secure the control under which it is lost, the greater is the intensity of the orgastic experience.

In short, the pleasure of genital orgasm is the consequence of a well-articulated experience of controlled loss of control. This is why, in human societies, sex is both a brutalizing and civilizing force.

* * *

In capitalist countries prostitution is condemned because it reminds people that everyone lives by renting some part of his body: manual workers rent their muscles, prostitutes their genitals. Prostitution and nonmarital sex also threaten the sexual monopoly of marriage and offer the prospect of a "free market" in erotic exchanges from which modern capitalist societies shrink in fear of freedom.

In communist countries prostitution is condemned because it reminds people that no one owns anything that he can rent. Since the state owns everything and everybody and since the state cannot copulate, the communist state is even more antagonistic toward prostitution than is the capitalist state.

* * *

Men seem to be fascinated by orgasm in women much more than women are by orgasm in men. The most likely reason for this is that male orgasm is readily equated with ejaculation, and that ejaculation, although not the same as orgasm, is clearly visible. This should tell people something about the connection between sex and secrecy, but they do not want to hear what it is.

* * *

Formerly, when the Western attitude toward sex was

puritanical, sexual organs and acts were, in effect, sacralized. The more completely they were sacralized, the more effectively was this use of such body parts discouraged. Thus, sexual pleasure was contingent on the successful profanation of something sacred.

Now, when the Western attitude toward sex is permissive, sexual organs and acts are, in effect, profaned. The more completely they are profaned, the more effectively is this use of such body parts encouraged. Thus, sexual pleasure is now contingent on the successful sacralization of something profane.

Men and Women

Formerly, women were considered "pure" only so long as they remained asexual; if they asserted themselves by engaging in and enjoying sexual activities, they became "dirty whores"—that is, impure, polluted, and taboo.

Mutatis mutandis, women are now considered "pure" only so long as they remain slender; if they assert themselves by engaging in and enjoying eating, they become "repulsively fat"—that is, impure, polluted, and taboo.

* * *

A spirited engine is a good engine, a spirited horse is a good horse, and a spirited man is a good man—but a spirited woman is a "masculine" woman. This is how the language of male chauvinism refracts "reality."

* * *

Men are identified by their achievements and occupations, women by their bodies and husbands; men by what they *do,* women by what they *are* or *have.* Thus, women are regularly identified by the size of their busts, waists, and hips, by how tall they are and how much they weigh, and by who they are married to. Hence, it is misleading to compare the situation of women only to that of oppressed minorities, such as Negroes or Jews. Women's status also resembles that of society's scapegoats—for example, that of addicts, homosexuals, insane criminals, and mental hospital patients generally —who are dehumanized by being defined as "nothing but" some of their (defective, deviant) qualities.

Accordingly, women should oppose as staunchly the ways in which they are misidentified by others, and often by themselves, as they oppose specific economic, legal, and political discriminations.

*   *   *

Could Jews publicly identified as Christians, or Christians as Jews, maintain and develop their own religious identity? The question strikes one as absurd. Yet women bearing their husbands' names, who are thus publicly identified as not themselves but as the wives of other persons, are now expected to maintain and develop their own individual identities. This unreasonable expectation is the consequence of two typical contemporary habits of minds. One is our disrespect for history, which, in this case, lulls us into believing that although in the past the wife's identity was supposed to have been submerged in that of her husband, now it can easily be separate from his. The other is our disrespect for language, which, in this case, encourages us to defy the wisdom of the ancient insight that "In the beginning was the Word, and the Word was with God, and the Word was God."*

*   *   *

In Genesis, God names all the creatures He has created, including the Jews; but most of those creatures can't name Him, and the Jews are explicitly forbidden to do so. In real life, men name women and sculpt, paint, and photograph them in the nude; but women are, in the

---

* John, 1:1.

main, forbidden to name even themselves, much less represent men in the nude. While women may thus be idolized, they are also objectified. And as an object cannot be an agent, it cannot be free.

* * *

A pessimistic history of one hundred years of women's emancipation from 1870 to 1970: from *Kinder, Kirche, Küche* (children, church, kitchen) to diets, drugs, doctors.

* * *

Men diet to live longer; women, to look better.

* * *

Men sell their souls for success and money; women, for acceptance and virtue. Having completed these transactions, they often fall into one another's arms, each hoping to regain what they have lost, each disappointed at finding the shelves empty and the cash register locked.

* * *

Traditionally, men used power to gain sex, and women used sex to gain power. The new ethic of equality between men and women must come down to one of two things: either, as the romantics hope, that neither men nor women will use power to gain sex; or, as the realists expect, that both men and women will use power to gain sex and sex to gain power.

* * *

Sexual politics is the subordination of personal preference to public pressure.

Thus, formerly, when men sought to adapt to the social requirements of male chauvinism, they often lived in fear of being shamed and stigmatized as homosexuals. Hence, many homosexual men hid their true sexual preferences behind a façade of publicly validated heterosexual performance: they married and fathered children. Their homosexuality remained a secret vice or was repressed altogether.

Now, when women seek to adapt to the social requirements of female chauvinism, they often live in fear of being shamed and stigmatized as heterosexuals. Hence, many heterosexual women now hide their true sexual preferences behind a façade of publicly validated homosexual performance: they loudly profess their lesbianism and flaunt their female lovers. Their heterosexuality remains a secret vice or is repressed altogether.

Ethics

The safest sin: envy, which is easily disguised as enthusiasm for equality.

The most dangerous virtue: tolerance, which is easily construed as sympathy for subversion.

* * *

The principle of tyranny: anyone not for me is against me.

The principle of tolerance: anyone not against me is for me.

* * *

The modern, liberal-scientific ethic: if it's bad for you, it should be prohibited; if it's good for you, it should be required.

* * *

The therapeutic ethic: punish and torture the innocent, and call it mental hospitalization; excuse and indulge the guilty, and call it the insanity defense.

* * *

Heresy: believing that the brain should be an organ generating new truths to please its owner instead of reproducing old falsehoods to please the authorities.

* * *

A person remains a child so long as he feels that he owes others the truth. He becomes an adolescent when he asks himself what he owes others and what others owe him. And he reaches adulthood when he concludes that others deserve the truth only if they are trustworthy and that he owes them the truth only in proportion as others prove themselves to be deserving of it.

* * *

Two wrongs don't make a right—but they make a first-rate justification for a third wrong.

* * *

To forgive all is to demand all.

* * *

Equality is the mirage of a well in the desert of domination and submission that comprises human relations. Those who expect to quench their thirst from it are destined to perish painfully.

* * *

Saliva is a watery mucoid secretion kept in the mouth; spittle is the same thing spit out. These common human phenomena epitomize the basis of most ethical judgments: what is inside is ours, is good; what is outside is not ours, is bad.

* * *

We possess appropriate terms to identify a variety of moral beliefs and the social organizations which seek to promote them—such as anarchism, communism, conservatism, liberalism, socialism, and so forth. The one moral belief for which we have no appropriate term is that which emphasizes the value of personal choice and the political forms that would promote such choice-making. I propose that we call this ethic, and the politics which

articulates it, *hereticalism* (making use of the Greek root
hairein, which means "to choose").

* * *

Jesus taught that we should "Render unto Caesar the
things that are Caesar's, and unto God the things that
are God's."* Implicit in what this parable omits is the
view that there are "no things that are ours" and hence
that there is nothing that we should render unto ourselves. Implicit in it, too, is the command that we ought
to live for Caesar and God, and not for ourselves; in
short, that the proper ethic is heteronomy, not autonomy.

* * *

Rules of conduct according to the ethics of autonomy:

Attack and criticize the oppressor, but do not humili-
ate him.

Defend and support the oppressed, but do not
glamorize him.

Respect and learn from everyone, regardless of merit
or position.

Bestow admiration and love because it is deserved,
not because you need others to protect and love you.

Know your enemies; avoid them, if you can; subdue
them, if you can't.

Honor your friends; be loyal to them, if you can; warn
them, if you can't.

* * *

If a person asked himself, "Who owns my income?" he
would have to reply: "This much of it, the federal government; this much of it, the state government; this
much of it the county (or city) government; and what's
left, I own—it is mine."

The answer to the question "Who owns my body?" is

* Matthew, 22:21.

similar. In part, a person's body is owned by the state; in part, by the medical profession; and what's left, he owns —it is his.

Thus, just as under the ethic of progressive taxation, the more money a person makes, the larger the share of his financial self-determination over which he loses control, so under the ethic of pharmacracy,† the more maladies he has, the larger the share of his bodily self-determination over which he loses control.

* * *

Marx and Freud: the two great Jewish anti-Semites. Marx, the communist, promoted the dictatorship of the proletariat; Freud, the psychoanalyst, promoted psychiatric imperialism. Each, in his own way, preached and practiced intolerance.

* * *

Serious men now seriously suggest that, to protect the American citizen's good health, the state should prohibit all advertising of nonprescription drugs like antacids and cough medicines; and that, to protect his freedom of speech, the state should permit every kind of erotic advertising and the public display of nude bodies and sexual acts.

* * *

In the United States today, the legal penalty for killing another person with poison may be less than it is for "poisoning" oneself with certain prohibited drugs. Nothing could more dramatically symbolize that we now regard heteronomy as sacred and autonomy as satanic.

* * *

"Property is theft," Proudhon declared, articulating a maxim that became the credo of Marxists and commu-

† For a definition of this term, see p. 180.

nists, and that prompted Shaw to declare it "the only perfect truism that has been uttered on the subject."‡

But suppose that a man goes into the mountains, brings back a piece of marble, and carves a beautiful statue out of it. He will have created property: he will "own" the statue and there will be others who will desire it for themselves. From whom has he stolen it? Truly, the anticapitalist mentality is more fanatical in its disregard of facts than any of the revealed religions had ever been.

* * *

Evil, observed Flannery O'Connor, "is not simply a problem to be solved, but a mystery to be endured."* Not until psychiatrists realize this and act accordingly, will the practice of psychiatry cease to be a moral affront, if not an obscenity.

* * *

The platonic maxim that "It is better to suffer wrong than to commit it" is fine for those to whom life is a spectator sport; the players, however, need something that gives them a little more protection in the clinches.

* * *

The maxim "Honesty is the best policy" is incomplete as it stands. Completed, it would read as follows: "Honesty is the best policy with those who are honest and the worst and stupidest policy with those who are dishonest."

* * *

All religions seem to originate, in part at least, in man's

‡ Shaw, G. B., *Maxims for Revolutionists* (1903), quoted in Stevenson, B., ed., *The Macmillan Book of Proverbs, Maxims, and Famous Phrases* (New York: Macmillan, 1948), p. 1899.

* Flannery O'Connor, "A Catholic Novelist in the Protestant South," in *Mystery and Manners* (New York: Farrar, Straus & Giroux, 1969), p. 209.

realization that life is full of pain and ends in decline
and death. The appeal of all religions thus rests, in part
at least, on promising man surcease from his tragic fate:
through a Messiah, a Savior, Paradise, Nirvana. Each of
the major religions promises that the sorrow of human
existence as we know it will be replaced if not by a posi-
tively joyful existence, then at least by relief from further suffering.

In the modern world, this function of religion—and not
only this one—has been replaced by science and psychiatry. Science, as scientism, promises a "better world" and
a "better life"—if only we "believe" in reason and practice its rituals. Similarly, psychiatry—as psychoanalysis,
psychotherapy, and mental healing in general—promises
the same results if only we "believe" in Freud, Menninger, Klein, Horney, the American Psychiatric Association, or some other psychiatric authority and if we practice his or her or its rituals.

It has long been obvious that the promises of religion
are fake. It should now be equally obvious that the
wholly similar promises of scientism—whether physical,
biological, or psychological—are equally fake. Does it
not follow, then, that a new ethic—fit for modern men
and women who know and accept all this—must be
based on the rejection of making false, unfulfillable
promises? What, then, must this ethic articulate and rit-
ualize as its highest value? Contract: that is, the value
of promising only what can be delivered and of deliver-
ing what is promised.

*   *   *

Ours is an age in which idols perish while idolaters
flourish. The result is liars worshiping the clothes of
naked emperors. The challenge is clear: we must
develop a new ethic of personal self-respect or sink into
another Dark Age of self-rejection.

Language

Ideologue: a person who uses ideas as incantations.

True believer: a person who accepts incantations as ideas.

Skeptic: a person who assumes that ideas are incantations until they are proven otherwise.

* * *

French structuralism: using words not as symbols but as decorations.

* * *

Inflation: demonetizing money.

* * *

Analogy is a conceptual instrument constructed by means of the proper arrangement of words, just as the microscope and the telescope are optical instruments constructed by means of the proper arrangement of lenses. If an object is too small or too far to be perceptible with the naked eye, we can often see it by viewing it through an optical instrument. In the same way, if an idea is emotionally too close or too far for us to perceive it, we can often see it by viewing it through an analogy.

*   *   *

To identify a person's face, a picture is said to be worth a thousand words. But to identify his soul, a word is worth a thousand pictures.

*   *   *

An aphorism stands in the same relation to a description as a caricature stands to a portrait.

*   *   *

Metaphor is a verbal cartoon—a caricature of an action, idea, object, or person. Hence, it must be grasped, not analyzed; explaining it destroys it; and to take it literally is to mistake a caricature for the idea or person caricaturized.

*   *   *

Metaphorization: making metaphors; those who make them—for example, poets, "psychotics," and psychiatrists —are metaphorists. The opposite of literalization.

*   *   *

Literalization of metaphor: mistaking metaphor for fact. For example: in Roman Catholicism, the belief that the Eucharist is the body and blood of Christ; in modern psychiatry, the belief that body and mind are one and the same thing or two faces of a single coin, and hence the further belief that mental illnesses (that is, deviations from moral norms) and bodily illnesses (that is, deviations from medical norms) are the same sorts of diseases.

*   *   *

"The lunatic, the lover, and the poet,/ Are of imagination all compact," said Shakespeare.* They are "all compact" of language too: each uses metaphors of his own creation in preference to those ready-made in his lan-

* *A Midsummer Night's Dream*, Act V, Scene 1, lines 7–8.

guage and society; and each uses his own language as an asylum where he seeks refuge from the Other and as a work of art with which he seeks to set himself above the Other.

How, then, do they differ from one another? Not in what they do, but in how well or poorly they do it; in how successful or unsuccessful they are as rhetoricians. The poet persuades many to see the world as he does; the lover, one; the lunatic, none.

* * *

"The greatest thing by far," says Aristotle, "is to be a master of metaphor. It is the one thing that cannot be learnt from others."† The human fear of freedom and love of dependence is perhaps nowhere displayed more tragically than in the one-sided application of this profound truth: those who create new metaphors with whose literalized interpretations they enslave others are acclaimed as great thinkers; whereas those who unravel metaphors with whose clarification they liberate others are dismissed as annoying eccentrics. Karl Marx and Sigmund Freud manufactured mystifying metaphors; Charles Peirce and Karl Kraus unmasked metaphors used as mendacities.

* * *

Using metaphor means primarily giving something a name that belongs to something else resembling it—for example, calling a remark "cutting" or a person "foxy." But there is another kind of metaphor, one based on a similarity not of appearance but of intention—for example, calling bread and wine the "body and blood of Jesus" or a disagreement a "disease." In the latter case, we use metaphor not to identify a similarity seemingly

† Aristotle, *De Poetica* (*Poetics*), translated by Ingram Bywater, in R. McKeon, ed., *The Basic Works of Aristotle,* (New York: Random House, 1941), p. 1479.

inherent in the objects but to create one between them for strategic purposes: by treating bread as if it were the body of a god, we generate certain similarities between it and the deity; by treating certain opinions as if they were the unintended consequences of an illness rather than the intentional products of a decision, we create certain similarities between deviance and disease. The languages of poetry and science make use of descriptive metaphors, whereas the languages of religion, politics, and psychiatry make use of strategic metaphors.

* * *

To the Jews, God is Lord, not lord; and a Lord cannot have a son, only a lord can. To the Christians, God is both Lord and lord; hence He can have a son who, himself, is both man and God, lord and Lord. The Jewish idea of God is thus pure metaphor; whereas the Christian idea of God is a combination of metaphor and literalized metaphor.

* * *

The Jews understood that God can remain a deity only so long as He has no name. Wanting to glorify such a deity, Moses founded a religion in which no name must be attached to God. This is called Judaism.

The Jews also understood that man can remain a person only so long as he has a good name. Wanting to vilify man, Freud founded a religion in which a vile name must be attached to every man, woman, and child. This religion is called "psychoanalysis."

* * *

"Homosexuality" is the name we give to the preference for sexual intercourse with members of one's own sex. If we called preference for marriage with members of one's own race and religion "homoraciality" and "homoreligiosity," would that make them mental diseases? Would the members of the American Psychiatric Association have to vote on whether or not they are mental diseases?

* * *

A kosher pickle is a pickle blessed by the rabbi. Holy matrimony is sex blessed by the priest. A mentally healthy person is a person blessed by the psychiatrist.

Pork is meat cursed by the rabbi. Fornication is sex cursed by the priest. The "schizophrenic" is a person cursed by the psychiatrist.

* * *

We only eat those things which we consider "good" and must therefore give them good names. When people call insects "insects" and rats "rats," they don't eat them. When they do eat them, as the Chinese did, they call grasshoppers "bushwood shrimp," and rats "household deer."‡

* * *

When a patient fakes illness, it's called "malingering," "hysteria," or "hypochondriasis"; when a healer fakes treatment, it's called "faith healing," "hypnosis," or "acupuncture." In the language of medicine, the same behavior is thus labeled differently, depending on whether the actor is sufferer or healer: the sufferer is demeaned and diagnosed; the healer is metaphorized and mythicized.

* * *

In the old language of state hospital psychiatry, "admission" meant imprisonment in an asylum, "treatment" meant torture, and so on. In the new language of community psychiatry, there are similar euphemisms: "release into the community" means forcing mental pa-

‡ See Reay Tannahill, *Food in History* (New York: Stein and Day, 1973), p. 152.

tients out of institutions that have become their homes; "community placement" means controlling their freedom of choice about where they can and cannot live; and so forth.

*   *   *

A person who feels sad may be said to be dejected or depressed. A person who claims to be God, may be said to be a boastful liar or a deluded schizophrenic. The difference between these descriptions is the same as the difference between calling a spade a shovel or an agricultural instrument for soil penetration.

*   *   *

What a poem translated into prose loses, a personal complaint translated into a medical symptom gains—namely, the power to make an emotional impact on an audience.

*   *   *

If a man tells his wife, "You are an angel, you make me the happiest man in the world," he is a loving husband; but if he tells her, "You are a witch, you are poisoning me!" then he is a lunatic.

The moral: metaphors of love and praise are music to our ears, but metaphors of hate and blame are madness to them.

*   *   *

Physicians and experts in the mental health field are fond of referring to nearly everyone as a "patient"—a linguistic habit that has gone largely unnoticed and unchallenged. But the change, especially if involuntary, from person to patient is similar to that from citizen to subject. We would not look lightly on politicians referring to people indiscriminately as their subjects; neither should we so look on physicians referring to people indiscriminately as their patients. It is for us—not for them—to say whether or when we want to relinquish our roles as citizens and persons and become subjects and patients.

* * *

The explanations mental patients give to their experiences are called "delusions" and "fantasies"; the explanations psychiatrists give to them are called "diagnoses" and "interpretations." In hospital psychiatry, the best way to tell the patient from the psychiatrist is by who has the keys; in nonhospital psychiatry, by who has the key words.

* * *

A person can feel sorry for himself or for someone else, but he can feel happy only for someone else. What does this fact—that, in English, a person cannot feel happy for himself—tell us about us? Two things: that self-pity is a more drastic and self-conscious experience than self-satisfaction; and hence, that, to many persons, self-pity may be more satisfying than self-satisfaction.

* * *

The history of the so-called temperance movement is the history of the abuse of the word "slavery." The puritanical foes of the nonmedicinal uses of drugs began, at the end of the nineteenth century, by claiming that as the "native races" had formerly been enslaved by white men, so they were then being enslaved by liquor. Then they extended their claim by maintaining that all persons everywhere who used substances of which they disapproved were "enslaved" by these substances. They thus metaphorized the word "enslaved," extending its use from literal slavery, which is something the subject, called "slave," does not want, to metaphorical slavery, which is something the subject, called "free citizen," wants only too much.

* * *

Had the white settlers in North America called the natives "Americans" instead of "Indians," they could not have said that "The only good Indian is a dead Indian" and could not have so easily deprived them of their lands and lives. Depriving individuals or groups of their proper names is often the first step in depriving them of their property, liberty, and life.

*   *   *

When the Swiss are for nonintervention in war, they are called "neutral"; when Americans are, they are called "isolationists."

*   *   *

Getting "dangerous drugs" from a doctor is called "drug treatment"; giving them to oneself is called "drug abuse."

Likewise, dying of a disease is called "natural death," but dying of a decision is called "suicide."

In these ways, and in countless others, our language says that heteronomy is good, and autonomy is evil. If we valued autonomy more and heteronomy less, we would call drug abuse "self-medication" and suicide "self-determined death."

*   *   *

Discussing psychiatric problems at international conferences with persons whose English is imperfect is like dueling with someone who grabs his sword by the blade: one is inhibited from pressing an intellectual argument on an interlocutor wounded by his very handling of the instrument of our communication.

*   *   *

Clear speech and writing betoken sincerity and respect for the rules of language and thus imply a willingness to eschew coercion by communication. Since the human larynx and tongue are actually used as claws and fangs, and words as venom, it is easy to understand why the unilateral verbal disarmament of semantic pacifism is both feared and admired.

* * *

Our body is composed of what we eat; our minds, of what we hear, read, say, and write. This is why every society, every social institution—religion, law, medicine—controls not only what we can and cannot take into our bodies, but also what we can and cannot take into our minds. In the final analysis, control of food is tantamount to control of the body, and control of language to control of the mind.

Classification

The men who wrote the Old Testament understood the meaning of classification as constraint. God was the classifier; everything He created—man, animals, plants, rocks—were the objects of His classification. Aptly, the Jewish God has no name, no image, no likeness. The Jews thus grasped that man's moral responsiveness, his sense of respect, is inversely proportional to his symbolic control over his moral ideal. The Jewish God is not a superman, like the gods of the Greeks were; nor is He a Father and a Son, as the Christian God is; He is not an "anything." The danger in this imagery is that it humiliates man. For millennia the Jews did indeed act as if they had been not God's Chosen People, but His most humble and humiliated folk. The Christians gave them something to be humble and humiliated about.

*　*　*

A driver pulls into a gas station. Why? One person will say because he is out of gas; another, because he wants some gas.

Many of the epistemological problems of the social sciences are epitomized by this example. To make progress, we must therefore distinguish between two types of explanations or behavior: the backward-looking or historical, and the forward-looking or teleological; the factual and the motivational; the "etiological" and the "therapeutic."

* * *

The less a person understands another, the greater is his urge to classify him—in terms of nationality, religion, occupation, or psychiatric status. Intimate acquaintance with another person renders such classification quite unnecessary. Categorizing and classifying people is a means not of knowing them better, but of making sure that we will not know them too well. In short, classifying another person renders intimate acquaintance with him quite unnecessary—and impossible.

Freedom and Slavery

The price of liberty is the loss of the love of paternalistic authority.

* * *

Freedom, in the psychological rather than political sense, is the ability to lie and get away with it, and yet not believe that one has told the truth. It is also the ability to tell the truth and not get away with it, and yet not believe that one has lied.

* * *

In the nineteenth century the great American railroads were built with government subsidies—and the achievement was attributed to "free enterprise." After the Second World War, the great American highway system was built with taxpayers' money—and the roads were called "freeways." It is evidently easier to use the word "free" as a self-enhancing epithet than as an accurate adjective.

* * *

Slavery is having to perform in a play written by someone else; freedom is having to write one's own play. Since most people don't even know how to spell, they find writing a play an insurmountable task, and hence prefer an insignificant role in a play written by someone else to no role at all.

*   *   *

Oppression is often real enough. But it is only one reason for not excelling in life; the other is that in the free marketplace of competition, one may be found wanting. This is why many persons prefer whining to working. By magnifying the crippling effects of oppression on personal destiny, they thus create the illusion that every Jew might be an Albert Einstein, every Negro a George Washington Carver, and every woman a Marie Curie.

*   *   *

How can men and women be free if they act like flies in a stable? After buzzing about briefly, they eagerly seek after sex, money, and power, to discover only too late that, like flies to flypaper, they are stuck to them.

*   *   *

Stanley Edgar Hyman correctly observes that Darwin tried "not to reduce man to a bestial condition, as opponents of [his] book charged, but to ennoble and humanize animals."* Similarly, Freud tried not to make the sane appear insane but rather the insane appear sane. In this respect, however, both failed: Darwin, because he recoiled from confronting the revealed religions; Freud, because he recoiled from confronting traditional psychiatry.

*   *   *

Freedom is opposed: in the name of God—by religion; in the name of the nation—by patriotism; in the name of

* Stanley Edgar Hyman, *The Tangled Bank: Darwin, Marx, Frazer, and Freud as Imaginative Writers* (New York: Antheneum, 1962), p. 50.

equality—by communism; in the name of social justice—by socialism; in the name of health—by therapeutism; in the name of mental health—by psychiatry; in the name of preventing suicide—by suicidology; in the name of drug controls—by drug abuseology. All those who so oppose freedom claim, of course, that they promote it; that only submission to their prohibitions constitutes "true" freedom.

* * *

One person's liberty may be enhanced at the expense of another's, as, for example, the master's is at the expense of the slave's. Thus liberty may be in conflict with liberty. It is not so with dignity. One person's dignity is never enhanced by another's indignity. Hence, in ordering our values, perhaps we should place dignity even above liberty.

* * *

Freedom is contingent on a legal system that treats unequals equally, whereas tyranny is contingent on one that treats equals unequally. Herein lies one of those paradoxes so characteristic of the human condition: namely, that decency and dignity may be obtained only through an impartiality verging on unmercifulness, and that barbarity and brutality may be gained most easily through a capriciousness rationalized as consideration for human differences.

The United States recognizes that its citizens have an inalienable right to leave their country. The United States therefore has no such problem as "defection."

Similarly, if the United States recognized that its citizens also have an inalienable right to self-medication (a right of which they were deprived in 1914), there would be no illegal inflow of heroin into the country. The United States would therefore have no such problem as "trafficking in dope."

Of course, some people would still take drugs some other people did not want them to take. But this would no more constitute "drug abuse" than leaving the country constitutes "border abuse."

In short, if a government believes that its citizens have no right to leave their country, it will generate policies which, in turn, will create the "problem of defection." Similarly, if a government believes that its citizens have no right to use "dangerous drugs," it will generate policies which, in turn, will create the "problem of drug abuse." Many national and social "problems" are thus created not by what people do, but by the way governments *define* what they do and by the policies which such definitions impose on rulers and ruled alike.

Confronted with such totalitarian laws, most people in the "free" world assert that the prohibitions are criminal and that the victims are the citizens whose freedom they curtail. Yet, confronted with similar therapeutic laws—which prohibit certain movements in the chemical and sexual, rather than in the geographical, sphere—most people in the "free" world assert that the prohibitions are merely unfortunate or unwise because they create "crimes without victims." This is self-deception of the worst sort: it is the unwillingness to see and acknowledge the malevolent tyranny of one's own rulers, and, where it applies, of one's own conscience, on whose behest a "free" people deprive themselves of a liberty whose burden they are too weak to bear.

* * *

The insanity defense and the insanity verdict are joined in unholy matrimony in the insanity trial. The defendant claims the nonexistent condition of insanity as an excuse for what he did to his victim; the court claims the same nonexistent condition as a justification for what it does to the defendant.

* * *

Right to privacy: a modern "liberal" interpretation of what the Founding Fathers had in mind, conveniently called a "constitutional right." Appeal to it enables American lawyers and jurists, politicians and journalists, to regard the surgical removal of a fetus from a woman's uterus in a hospital as a "private act," protected by this right—and the self-administration of amphetamine or marijuana in the home as not such an act and hence unprotected by it.

Punishment

Formerly, when priests ruled and people exalted the spirit, the favorite methods of punishments were breaking men's bodies on the rack and the wheel. Today, when physicians rule and people exalt the body, our favorite punishments are breaking men's minds with drugs, electrical convulsions, and surgical amputations of the brain.

* * *

Perhaps nothing illustrates the death of individualism as dramatically as the agitation for the abolition of the death penalty. Here is why.

Central to the ideology of individualism is this dual proposition: first, that the person should be sovereign over himself and, so long as he eschews force and fraud, in his dealings with others; and, second, that the state should exercise a monopoly over force to discharge its primary duty, the protection of the individual from internal and external enemies.

Those who would abolish the death penalty would allow the individual the "right" (in the sense of "opportunity") to kill, but would deprive the state of this right. At the same time, those who most ardently advocate the

abolition of the death penalty usually support arrangements that give the state a monopoly over activities in
which it has no legitimate business at all, such as gambling.

The upshot is a society that prohibits individuals from
engaging in gambling as a business, but promotes gambling as a philanthropy when conducted by the state;
and that prohibits the state from killing, even in self-
defense, while allowing the individual to engage in such
violence, by giving him another chance to kill, in or out
of prison.

*   *   *

Prisons are now called "correctional institutions" in
which the inmates are "rehabilitated." Madhouses are
called "mental hospitals" in which the inmates are
"treated." Our society, in effect, declares its collective
disbelief in punishment; and it is then astonished that
crime flourishes and that institutional inmates feel that
they are the victims of cruel and unusual punishments.

Control and Self-Control

Self-control and self-esteem vary directly: the more self-esteem a person has, the greater, as a rule, is his desire, and his ability, to control himself.

The desire to control others and self-esteem vary inversely: the less self-esteem a person has, the greater, as a rule, is his desire, and his ability, to control others.

* * *

Parents teach their children discipline for two different, indeed diametrically opposite, reasons: to render the child submissive to them and to make him independent of them. Only a self-disciplined and self-controlled person can be reliably obedient; and only such a person can be autonomous and independent of authority. This is the reason for the seeming paradox that the most active, energetic, and independent people—like the Americans, Germans, and Japanese—are also the most obedient and submissive.

* * *

To avoid the burden of self-control, people hire politicians to mutilate their liberties and physicians to mutilate their bodies. When they realize how seriously they have been injured, people still do not usually assume self-control, but instead hire more politicians and physicians and submit themselves to even more radical mutilations—all in the vain hope that they can "purify" themselves by rejecting the "pollution" of autonomy and that they can do this short of political or physical suicide.

* * *

Nonsexual pleasures derive either from the gratification of a need for control, as in games, sports, and other activities requiring the active mastery of skills; or from the gratification of a need for loss of control, as in sleep, religion, and intoxication with certain drugs. Genital orgasm among some adults in certain contemporary cultures seems to be distinguished among human pleasures by successfully combining, in a single context and act, the gratifications of both activity and passivity, of control and loss of control.

* * *

There are three basic ways of controlling human beings: by force, by exploiting weakness and dependence, and by money. Each of these systems of controls is institutionalized: force in the military; exploiting weakness and dependence in religion; and money in business. As these institutions become oppressive, each is opposed by an ideology or institution intended to protect the victim, each protection becoming in turn a fresh source of danger: force is opposed by pacifism, leaving man unprotected against anarchy; religion is opposed by atheism, leaving man unprotected against anomie; and the free market is opposed by communism, leaving man unprotected against the state.

* * *

Homicide is to suicide as rape is to masturbation.

* * *

Until recently, most psychiatrists, psychologists, and other behavioral scientists wholeheartedly approved and supported the "behavioral controls" of medicine and psychiatry. Now many of them are beginning to criticize some of these "controls." But most of these men and women remain as hostile to individual freedom and responsibility as they have always been. They now demand more "controls"—that is, professional and governmental controls—over "behavioral controls." This is like first urging a person to drive over icy roads at breakneck speed to get over them as fast as possible and then, when his car goes into a skid, advising him to apply his brakes. Whether because they are stupid or wicked or both, such persons invariably recommend less controls where more are needed (for example, in relation to punishing offenders), and more controls where less are needed (for example, in relation to contracts between consenting adults).

Personal Conduct

Reason: the capacity to weigh and make choices; what distinguishes human beings from animals, and what human beings use to deny the validity of this distinction.

* * *

Greatness: the willingness to risk exposing one's littleness.

* * *

The trouble with having both feet on the ground is that it brings one into unbearably close contact with the world.

* * *

The golden mean between the ridiculous and the sublime is often the absurd.

* * *

There are no universal geniuses; there are only universal fools.

* * *

Usually it is painful to be wrong; sometimes it is fatal to be right.

* * *

There is no good digestion without hydrochloric acid; and no good thinking without adrenalin.

* * *

As the price of liberty is vigilance—so the price of independence is self-determination, the price of dignity is self-assertion, and the price of respect is self-respect.

* * *

The masochist lives by the maxim that it is better to be wanted as a victim than not to be wanted at all.

* * *

You can't teach an old dog new tricks; but you can an old man. That's one of the differences between dogs and persons.

* * *

Craftsmanship is submission to the authority of excellence. In proportion as authority is nowadays confused with force and rejected as illegitimate, craftsmanship is displaced by poor workmanship. Through his good works, the proud craftsman displays his love of the Other. Through his shoddy work, the humiliated worker displays his hatred of the Other. Each, in his own way, reaffirms his identity—as submissive but free, and as rebellious but enslaved.

* * *

Genius is the ability to see with the eyes of the child and to reason and write about what one sees with the mind and mastery of the adult.

The opposite of genius is the bureaucrat, who sees with the eyes of the adult, reasons with the mind of the child, and writes with the style of the dead.

* * *

If a person's possessions are stolen, he is expected to feel injured because he has been robbed; but if his ideas are stolen, he is expected to feel flattered because he is being imitated. Clearly, people value things more highly than thoughts—probably because everyone can have things which they therefore want protected, but not everyone can have ideas which they therefore feel ready to leave unprotected.

* * *

As a person unaccustomed to exercising his muscles develops a Charley horse when he begins to exercise them, so a person unaccustomed to exercising his will develops, when he begins to exercise it, a spiritual Charley horse. And as the one must bear the literal Charley horse of his body, if he wants to enhance its power to overcome physical obstacles, so the other must bear the metaphorical Charley horse of his mind, if he wants to enhance its power to overcome spiritual obstacles.

* * *

We speak of avoiding responsibility for acts for which we are responsible as "making excuses" for ourselves. But we have no analogous expression for assuming responsibility for acts for which we are not responsible. Actually, people often engage in both kinds of conduct—making excuses for themselves to gain material ends and making accusations against themselves to gain spiritual ends.

* * *

Psychological independence is contingent on economic independence, and economic independence is contingent on a free market. This is why those most economically independent are generally also the most mentally independent; why the self-employed are more psychologically independent than those employed by the state or by large private organizations; why capitalism stimulates, while communism stifles, personal independence; and why, under communism, only the artists—who sometimes manage to remain psychologically self-employed even when they are paid by the state—retain their spiritual independence.

*   *   *

In proportion as a person feels that his life possesses meaning, he tends to be patient, and in proportion as he feels that it lacks meaning, he tends to be impatient. This is why, in the face of what may seem as a manifest "waste of time," it is the busy person who is often patient, and the idle one who is impatient. The reason for this seeming paradox is that for the person who feels usefully engaged in life, a "waste of time" is often a welcome change of pace and a pleasant relaxation; whereas for the person who feels uselessly adrift in life, a "waste of time" is an exacerbation of his customary inactivities and a painful reminder of what his whole life is.

*   *   *

Both psychiatrists and laymen use the word "panic" to refer to two quite different things: first, to the fear of what the person himself might do (the fear of "falling apart"); and second, to the fear of what others might do to him (the fear of being attacked). These two situations differ in the same way as the fear of going bankrupt differs from the fear of being robbed. Each calls for a very different sort of preparation for proper protection.

*   *   *

Habits in personal conduct are like energy in physics: so long as we remain alive, we cannot get rid of habits by annihilating them, by making them disappear; we can only change or transform one habit into another. Moreover, there are two basic patterns or types of habit transformations. In one, the person relinquishes one habit by adopting its opposite; for example, the alcoholic becomes a teetotaler; the obese person starves himself or herself; the devoutly religious person becomes a devout atheist. In the other type, the person relinquishes one habit by adopting another habit similar to it; for example, the smoker switches from cigarettes to pipe to chewing gum, the obese person from food to cigarettes or from high-caloric to low-caloric foods; the orthodox Jew becomes an orthodox psychoanalyst, the zealous Christian, a zealous communist.

* * *

During adolescence, temptations are numerous and the demands to resist them stringent. As we grow older, the temptations diminish and the opportunities to give in to them increase. And so we arrive at old age, with only one temptation left: to die, and with neither reason nor will to resist it.

* * *

Young people are afraid to die. Older people often realize, when it is too late, that they were afraid to live. This is why many of them do not really want either to live or to die.

* * *

There are three types of self-love. In order of increasing intensity, they are: self-love unconcealed, self-love concealed as the love of others, and self-love concealed as self-hate. The first is called "self-esteem" by the subject, "self-assurance" by the lay observer, and "narcissism" by the psychoanalyst. The second is called "love" by the subject, "altruism" by the lay observer, and "maturity" by the psychoanalyst. The third is called "inferiority" by the subject, "stupidity" by the lay observer, and "masochism" by the psychoanalyst.

Sooner or later the self-love of a person comes into conflict with the self-love of others with whom he interacts. The more intense the self-loves, the more frequent and explosive are the conflicts between them.

＊　＊　＊

To survive as an individual, a person must learn how to say small noes often and skillfully. Those who fail to learn how to do this are, in desperation, often driven to saying a big no once and for all: they are then categorized as psychiatrically depressed or schizophrenically withdrawn, when in fact they merely find it easier to say no once loudly than many times softly.

＊　＊　＊

Few people now doubt that violent acts are motivated by aggressiveness and that persons who commit such crimes are aggressive. It seems obvious enough. But it is not so simple.

How much human food consumption is motivated by a physiological need for nutrition? How much erotic activity is motivated by a biological urge for sexual satisfaction? In each case, surely, only a part of it, and often a small part. Similarly, a good deal of criminal activity is motivated not by aggression, but by a desire to relieve boredom, to create excitement, to call attention to oneself, to achieve at least temporary fame and glory and success. The whole idea of attributing crime, and of course war as well, to aggression, and hence the search for their "solution" in the control of aggression—which is now an unquestioned assumption in intellectual discourse and social science—is, in my opinion, fundamentally mistaken.

＊　＊　＊

A fundamental motive for personal conduct is the desire to avoid boredom or its derivative, the desire to have something to live for. To satisfy this urge, men and women turn to food and drink, sex and work, crime and conquest. In general, creating trouble for others is one of the most popular ways people seek to avoid boredom; creating trouble for themselves is a close second. Creating meaning in less destructive, less cheaply dramatic, ways is more difficult and more rare.

* * *

Life is potentially a big empty hole, and there are few more satisfying ways of filling it than by striving for and achieving excellence.

Social Relations

Impertinence: the name which authorities give to the aspirations for, and declarations of, independence of their inferiors.

* * *

The two principal monomanias of modern man: monotheism and monogamy.

* * *

What is a friend? For some, a partner for playing *folie à deux;* for others, a sympathetic but incorruptible judge of one's judgments.

* * *

Life is not a bowl full of cherries; it's a bowl full of ironies.

* * *

If a person feels sorry for himself, others will give him something to be sorry for.

* * *

Beware of feeling sorry for someone who can hurt you and is likely to do so if given a chance. Compassion of this sort is a luxury only the very powerful or the very masochistic can afford.

*   *   *

In religion, the supreme value is inflexibility, which the faithful call "consistency"; in politics, the supreme value is inconsistency which the loyal call "flexibility."

*   *   *

Articulate persons argue. Inarticulate persons quarrel and, because they are unable to argue, mistake argumentation for quarreling.

*   *   *

Animals kill animals of different species for meat. Human beings kill other human beings—and avoid killing certain animals—for metaphors.

*   *   *

In academia, the rule is, publish or perish; in bureaucracies, it's proliferate or perish; in drug abuseology, it's persecute or perish.

*   *   *

If you have strongly held opinions, you are opinionated; if you don't, you lack conviction; either way, there is something wrong with you.

*   *   *

Great jurists are made by sacrificing plaintiffs to the Constitution; great physicians, by sacrificing patients to Research.

The moral: If you value your freedom and health, don't be a test case, either in the courts or in the clinics.

*   *   *

In traditional American capitalism, people are moti-vated, and are expected to be motivated, by the desire to "keep up with the Joneses." In modern Scandinavian socialism, they are motivated, and are expected to be motivated, by the desire to "keep the Jacobsens from getting ahead of them."

* * *

Beware of people who tell you that a little knowledge is a dangerous thing—unless they quickly add that no knowledge is a fatal thing. They are trying to make you more vulnerable, not more wise.

* * *

Beware of the person who, in his relations with you, acts as if he had no duties or obligations to you. He is a rapist, literally or metaphorically: he will treat you as an object of his desires—to satisfy his lust for self-gratification.

Beware of the person who, in his relations with you, acts as if you had no duties or obligations to him. He is a therapist, literally or metaphorically: he will treat you as an object of his duties—to satisfy his lust for self-esteem.

* * *

Insofar as raising crops and children does not consume all of the energies of human beings, there remains "excess time" which people must find ways of using or killing. Religion and warfare, art and addiction, and many other human activities might thus be seen, in part, as dramatic performances for a bored but theater-loving audience.

* * *

"All the world's a stage,/ And all the men and women merely players." If we take this metaphor seriously—that is, if we regard social existence as being a play performed by actors before an audience—then it follows that people must be either on the stage or off it. To the question, "Who should be on stage and who should be off it?" different political systems give different answers.

Bygone feudal societies offered a rigid set of rules concerning who should be on the stage and who in the audience.

Modern capitalist societies offer the absurd promise that, if everyone is decent and diligent, everyone can be on the stage.

Modern communist societies—perhaps partly in response to the insoluble problem posed by the challenge of this global seating arrangement—shut down the theater. Instead of coercing the masses into the audience, as traditional societies have done through the ages, and instead of trying to accommodate ever more people on a stage so overcrowded as to render it increasingly unattractive, as modern "free" societies have done, the communists order everyone out of the building and into the fields and factories, there to labor for the creation of a society in which no one knows what theaters and plays are and hence in which no problem can arise as to who should be on the stage and who in the audience.

* * *

In intimate and lasting human relations, psychological autonomy and physical proximity vary inversely. Those who foolishly want to maximize both—for example, in marriage or friendship—will have neither; whereas those who wisely are satisfied with one or the other, or some of each sometimes—as married people used to be and as friends now tend to be—may have one or the other or sometimes some of each.

* * *

The goods and services a person has to offer another shape his social relations. Among these offerings, the most important are care, affection, money, food, sex, and artistic or intellectual pleasure. Some of these offerings are more highly valued than others; and sometimes some are valued negatively, in accordance with the moral premise that a person should be valued not for what he or she has to offer but for "himself" or "herself." In modern societies, for example, those who supply money are valued more highly than those who supply food, and those who supply entertainment are valued more highly still. Further, women valued for their beauty are regarded as "sexual objects," whereas men valued for their intelligence are not regarded as "brain objects." In this view, it is wrong to value a Marilyn Monroe only for her body, but it is not wrong to value an Albert Einstein only for his brain. This inconsistency reveals not only the profoundly antisexual and pro-intellectual character of the moral underpinnings of our social relations, but also our persistent denial of the fact that we value people not for "themselves" but for what they "offer" us.

* * *

It is fashionable nowadays to assert that if one person "uses" another, the true humanity of both is violated; and hence that, in a morally proper relationship, a person should not "use" another. This is idealistic self-deception. People always use each other. Human relationships are good or bad, moral or immoral, depending not on whether people use each other, but on how they do so.

* * *

There is endless speculation in psychiatry and the social sciences about whether lawbreakers should be punished or treated; about whether punishment may not be therapeutic and treatment punitive. This is another pseudoproblem which disappears if we define "treatment" and "punishment" not in terms of their outcomes but solely in terms of their voluntariness or involuntariness. Treatments are then those interventions which the subject—called "patient"—seeks or submits to freely (in exchange, he hopes, for a release from illness); whereas punishments are those interventions which the subject—called "prisoner"—does not seek and submits to by force (in exchange, he hopes, for release from further punishment). Not surprisingly, the outcome of either intervention may be judged beneficial or harmful by the subject himself or others; but neither the outcome nor its judgment should confuse us about the nature of the events that preceded it.

* * *

Problems of deviance are susceptible to only two types of adjustment: repression or tolerance. In other words, those who define "deviance" and are disturbed by it must coerce the deviants into conformity or kill them; or they must learn to tolerate them and live with them. There is no other choice.

Politics

Work is pushing matter around. Politics is pushing people around.

* * *

In the classic tale about the emperor's finely woven clothes, a child discovers that the emperor is unclothed. That makes him a naked emperor. But, for modern man, the point of this story should be not that the emperor is naked, but that he is a liar.

* * *

To control people—to rule over them—it is necessary to establish that those who govern are dignified and respect themselves and that those who are governed are undignified and do not respect themselves. The primary aim of every political ideology—of the imagery underlying every system of human organization—is to articulate that this distinction and division is true and just. The priests have maintained that the rulers are divine and the ruled diabolical; the politicians, that the rulers are competent and the ruled incompetent; and the physicians and psychiatrists, that the rulers are healthy and sane, and the ruled sick and insane. Then, offering to "care" and "guide" their depraved, dependent, diseased, or deranged brothers and sisters, each of these groups has been able, over long periods, to rule over their fellow men and women. Thus, in every political system, the most subversive idea is dignity and the most subversive act is a display of self-respect.

*   *   *

"Property is theft," said Proudhon. That is patent nonsense. Yet organized rule *is* thievery, the identity of the thief varying with the identity of the ruler. When monarchs ruled, kings and nobles robbed the people; when priests ruled, popes and pastors robbed the people; and now that scientific and medical authorities rule, researchers and physicians rob the people.

*   *   *

Masses of men can be, and can feel, equally poor, but they cannot be, and cannot feel, equally rich. Hence, the greater the value of equality in human affairs and the more it displaces and outranks such other values as liberty, responsibility, and justice, the more intense the pressure it exerts towards the adoption of socialist and communist types of political systems. Herein lies the basis for what Ludwig von Mises called the "anticapitalist mentality."

*   *   *

In nations, as in families, those who would rule by authority alone will fail because they lack force, and those who would rule by force alone will fail because they lack authority. This is because those subject to power, whether citizens or children, are exquisitely perceptive of what their rulers fear and try to avoid. They thus realize that those rulers who want to rely solely on authority shun force as if it were a symbol of tyranny; hence, these subjects lose respect for authority. Likewise, they realize that those rulers who want to rely solely on force shun authority as if it were a symbol of weakness; hence, these subjects lose respect for force.

Herein lies the explanation for the paradox of why people in free societies respect force more than authority; why people in totalitarian societies respect authority more than force; and why, in each, people endow with force those who wield authority and with authority those who wield force.

*   *   *

There is now an inverse relationship between the state's interests in and efforts to protect people from other people and from themselves: the more politicians protect people from harming themselves, the more they fail to protect them from being harmed by others. The upshot is a system of government ever more zealous to protect the people from driving cars without seatbelts, riding on motorcycles without crash helmets, and eating or drinking substances containing cyclamates, while leaving them ever more unprotected against murderers and muggers, rapists and robbers.

*   *   *

In every revolution, we may discern the following stages in the relations between oppressor and oppressed:

The oppressed feels envious of the oppressor and wants to dislodge him from power.

As the oppressor accommodates to the "legitimate demands" of the oppressed, the latter feels contempt for his adversary's compassion and co-operation.

As the oppressed gains equality, he is overcome with feelings of righteous indignation over the historical wrongs inflicted on him by his oppressors.

Superiority by the formerly oppressed leads either to the capitulation and withdrawal from the conflict of the former oppressor or to his guilty assumption of the role of the oppressed.

The stage for a new cycle of "revolutionary liberation" is now set.

* * *

All major political movements and ideologies that have inspired and moved masses of men are based not on the assertion of any "truths," but on the denial of one or more of man's fundamental passions, a denial which flatters people by making them seem better than they know they are. Christianity is, perhaps, the sole exception; but its ruthlessly honest appraisal of human nature is compromised by the promise of eventual salvation.

Here, in thumbnail sketches, are the characteristic denials of some important ideologies and "isms":

Anarchism: denial that competitive games require umpires.

Capitalism: denial that man does not live by money alone.

Communism: denial of autonomy, of the urge to "own" oneself and, by extension, property.

Conservatism: denial of the human propensity toward boredom and stupidity.

Feminism: denial of the conflict between demeaning men and depending on them.

Liberalism: denial of envy.

Libertarianism: denial of dependence and childishness.

Male chauvinism: denial of the conflict between demeaning women and depending on them.

Marxism: denial of the human limitations and passions of the proletariat.

Nationalism: denial of the similarities between one people and its neighbors, of the possible superiority of other people.

Pacifism, One-Worldism: denial of aggression, of the passion for domination.

Psychoanalysis: denial of dignity, mystery, tragedy, and faith.

Rousseauism, Noble-Savageism: denial of everything ignoble in man.

Socialism: denial of adventurousness and competitiveness.

* * *

Varieties of tyranny:

Political: the authorities expropriate all freedom; they enslave the people.

Economic: the authorities expropriate all property; they impoverish the people.

Pharmacological: the authorities expropriate all drugs; they incapacitate the people.

Scientific: the authorities expropriate all definitions; they confuse the people.

* * *

The two principal enemies of the individual in the modern world are communism and psychiatry. Each wages a relentless war against that which makes a person an individual: communism against the ownership of property; psychiatry against the ownership of the mind and body. Thus, the communists criminalize the autonomous use of money and commodities and reserve their greatest penalties for those "trafficking" in the black market, especially in foreign currencies; the psychiatrists criminalize the autonomous use of the mind, the sexual organs, and other body parts and reserve their greatest penalties for those "trafficking" in psychoactive drugs, especially in heroin.

* * *

No person, and especially no politician, is God's gift to

humanity; but some people, and many politicians, are surely the devil's gift. Representative governments are thus successful not in proportion to how well the voters select virtuous politicians, who are rare—but to how well they avoid wicked ones, who are common.

* * *

Before the twentieth century, autocratic regimes were typically corrupt, and this made life in them livable. The peculiar horror of our age is the incorruptible totalitarian leader. Incorruptibility on the parts of politicians would be desirable only in a society governed perfectly by perfect rules of law. In short, what the bribe is to politics, sacrifice is to religion. The incorruptible politician, like the deity immune to propitiation by sacrifice, is therefore more to be dreaded than desired.

* * *

There are three kinds of critics and opponents of arbitrary power or oppression.

The first—exemplified by Marx, Lenin, and the communists—want to take power away from the oppressors and give it to the oppressed, as a class.

The second—exemplified by Robespierre in politics and Rush in medicine, and their liberal, radical, and medical followers—want to take power away from the oppressors and give it to themselves.

The third—exemplified by Socrates, Emerson, and the modern free-market economists—want to take power away from the oppressors and give it to the oppressed, as individuals, for each to do with it as he pleases, but, it is hoped, for his own self-control.

Clearly, although countless men say they love liberty, only those who, by their actions, fall into the third group, mean it; the others merely want to replace a hated oppressor by a loved one, having usually themselves in mind for the job.

* * *

Ideologies and the political arrangements they sustain are, perhaps most importantly, systems of justification. Thus, in sacerdotalism, what justifies privileges is priestly power: the high-ranking clergy have access to wealth and women denied to others; in capitalism, it is economic power: the upper classes have access to goods and services denied to others; in communism, it is political power: the political leaders have access to goods and services denied to others; and in therapeutism it is medical power: physicians and patients have access to drugs and medical excuses denied to others.

* * *

In the United States today it is precisely those people who are most vocal in condemning the government for its management of the war in Vietnam who are also the most vocal in commending the government as the proper manager of our medical problems. The paradox is more apparent than real: the advocates of these policies are actually quite clear and consistent in their basic aim—the destruction of the nation they despise, which happens to be their own. James Burnham has accurately diagnosed this determination and called it the "suicide of the West."* This phrase is memorable but misleading. It identifies what is happening. But it ignores that the destroyers feel, and in fact are, profoundly dis-identified from their own country and its core values and are usually identified with its ideological enemies and their values; hence, their deed—the "killing" of their own moral tradition and political institutions—is more like patricide than suicide.

* James Burnham, *Suicide of the West: An Essay on the Meaning and Destiny of Liberalism* (New Rochelle, N.Y.: Arlington House, 1964).

Religion

The world—everything and everyone in it—is in a process of constant change. It is this fact, even more than that of personal death, which is intolerable to man. To create islands of permanence in a sea of change, men invent images and institutions of permanence: promises and contracts, mythologies and religions, traditions, institutions, and laws. Among all of these, God—the idea of a Creator who always was and always will be—is the single most powerful symbol of permanence. In the modern world, this symbol is threatened with displacement by the image of Science—the idea of Laws that have always been and will always be and which govern the movement of every particle of matter everywhere in the universe.

* * *

The Jews say God created the world in six days and rested on the seventh, which was Saturday. The Christians assert the same thing, but say the seventh day was Sunday. I wonder why God, if He is all-powerful, had to rest at all? And how, in the face of the blue laws, Americans can continue to believe that the United States is a secular society in which Church and State are separate?

* * *

God neither failed nor died, but was murdered. His killers, who have usurped His place, use as their fronts the two unquestionably legitimate enterprises of the modern age: the State and Science. Two of His assassins are Marx and Freud, one of whom characterized religion as "opium," and the other as a "neurosis." Thus, in the hands of the communists, religion freely professed becomes a dangerous drug that must be outlawed—and religion brutally enforced becomes Scientific Marxism which the whole world must embrace; while in the hands of the psychiatrists, religion freely professed becomes an illness that must be prevented or cured—and religion brutally enforced becomes a treatment to which the whole world must submit.

Medicine

When we assert that someone has a disease or has been diagnosed (voluntarily or involuntarily) as having a disease, we mean two quite different—indeed, from a legal and political point of view, two diametrically opposite—things.

First, asserting that someone has a disease is like asserting that he has money, in that we believe, and conduct ourselves as if we believed, that what the person does with his disease is his business. When the concept of disease is used in this way, it follows that physicians give treatment not so much because the patient has a disease, but rather because he seeks and authorizes treatment for it.

Second, asserting that someone has a disease is like asserting that he has committed a crime, in that we believe, and conduct ourselves as if we believed, that what the person does with his disease is not his business but the community's. When the concept of disease is used in this way, it follows that physicians, who are paid by and owe their loyalty to the community whom the patient endangers with his illness, give treatment not so much because the patient has a disease, but rather because the physician is commanded, perhaps even compelled, by the community to treat the patient, whether the patient likes it or not.

In short, as there are two radically different types of economic and political systems—one capitalist and free, the other communist and unfree; and as there are two radically different types of medical interventions, both called "treatment"—one voluntary and the other involuntary; so there are also two concepts of disease, each assuming that the patient suffers from whatever physicians believe constitutes a disease—one viewing disease as something over which the patient is sovereign, the other viewing it as something over which the community (the state) is sovereign.

* * *

What "a thing means," according to Charles Peirce, "is simply what habits it involves. . . . Thus, we come down to what is tangible and practical, no matter how subtle it may be; and there is no distinction of meaning so fine as to consist in anything but a possible difference of practice."[*]

Hence, if we begin with a word that denotes only a few practices and develop new practices which we still call by the same name, we shall make it impossible to speak clearly about what these new practices are. This has happened dramatically in medicine. For a long time, "disease" was something of which the patient complained and "treatment" something which he wanted done to him. With the growth of medical science and medical skill during the past century, new habits of behavior—on the part of both ordinary people and physicians—were subsumed under the old terms of "dis-

---

[*] Charles S. Peirce, "How to Make Our Ideas Clear," in Philip P. Wiener, ed., *Values in a Universe of Chance: Selected Writings of Charles S. Peirce (1839–1914)*, pp. 113–36 (Garden City, N.Y.: Doubleday Anchor, 1958), p. 123.

ease" and "treatment." For example, people complaining to physicians about other people became the disease called "psychosis"; and physicians doing things to people which they did not want done to them became the involuntary treatments called "electroshock" and "lobotomy."

* * *

The concepts of killing and murder stand in the same relation to each other as do the concepts of having a disease and being a patient. Today, most people understand the differences between a person having been killed and having been murdered or between a person being a killer and being a murderer; but few people understand the differences between having a disease and being a patient, between being sick and being in the sick role. The extent to which this analogy falls flat is a measure of the injury which modern medical thinking has inflicted on our understanding of human rights and responsibilities.

Killing and sickness are facts; murder and patienthood are ascriptions or roles. Thus, a person may be killed, for example, by lightning, without having been murdered; and a person may be considered to be a murderer, for example, when an innocent person is accused of murder, without having killed anyone. Similarly, a person may be sick, for example, suffering from hypertension without knowing it, and not be a patient; and a person may be considered to be a patient, for example, by faking illness to avoid the draft or obtain damages for alleged injuries, without being ill.

* * *

What justifies a therapeutic intervention—that is, an action by an individual called "physician" taken vis-à-vis the person or body of an individual called "patient"?

To the true believer in medicine, it is the disease

which the alleged patient has; to the medical autocrat, and to those who believe in him, it is the physician's judgment that the patient needs the treatment and that he—or his family or society—would benefit from it; to the loyal physician-employee of the Therapeutic State, and to those who believe in him, it is the decision of the government; and to the libertarian, it is the consent of the would-be patient.

Overlooking or confusing these conflicting moral and political premises and perspectives is the source of most of our so-called problems in medical ethics.

*   *   *

Further advances in the epistemology and ethics of medicine now depend on our willingness to articulate and acknowledge who controls various medical situations and whose aims they serve. This sort of medical self-disclosure would result in categories such as the following: personal medicine, for medicine under the control of the patient; scientific medicine, for medicine under the control of the medical profession; clerical or theological medicine, for medicine under the control of the priesthood or deities; police medicine, for medicine in the service of the police; executionary and military medicine, for medicine used for killing; forensic medicine, for medicine in the interests of law enforcement; entrepreneurial medicine, for medicine as a free trade; socialized medicine, for medicine as a state-controlled trade; and so forth.

In short, we need to identify various branches of medicine not only according to the kinds of patients treated, as in pediatric or geriatric medicine, but also according to the party that defines, in terms of its own interests, the language, scope, and methods of the field.

*   *   *

The subtle but pervasive influence of ethics and politics

on medicine is perhaps best revealed by the particular medical myths of dangerousness that characterize various periods.

In the nineteenth century, when individualism and self-control were the dominant values, the major medical myth of dangerousness was the belief that certain morally and legally prohibited activities injured the brain and the mind: in short, they caused nervous breakdowns. Thus, continence and masturbation were condemned because the medical profession claimed that they caused mental damage.

In the twentieth century, when collectivism and racism are the dominant values, the major medical myth of dangerousness is that certain morally and legally prohibited activities injure the genes and hence the health of future generations: in short, they cause chromosomal breakups. Thus, marijuana and LSD are condemned because the medical profession claims that they cause genetic damage.

The major medical mendacities of every age are thus symptomatic of the values which that age is most anxious to promote.

❋ ❋ ❋

What is the difference between physicians and veterinarians? From the descriptive or scientific point of view, the difference is that the physician treats human diseases or sick people, whereas the veterinarian treats animal diseases or sick animals; from the moral and political point of view, the difference is that the physician is (or ought to be) the agent of persons who choose to be his patients, whereas the veterinarian is the agent of persons who own sick animals. In proportion, then, as the physician becomes the agent of the State and in proportion as the State is totalitarian, the physician becomes, from a moral and political point of view, a "veterinarian": he is the agent of the State which owns its citizens, just as the veterinarian is the agent of the farmer who owns his animals. This is why killing animals is part of the normal function of the veterinarian, and why killing people is part of the normal function of the physician employed by the totalitarian state.

*   *   *

The tragedy of modern "scientific" medicine is that what physicians have gained in competence they have lost in compassion. Formerly, physicians could cure little and hence had to comfort much. Hence, too, physician and patient wanted the same thing: the patient wanted to receive medical ministration and the physician wanted to dispense it. The trouble then was that the physician was rich in compassion but poor in competence.

Today, physicians can cure more and hence want to comfort less. Hence, too, physician and patient now often want quite different things: the patient wants to receive comfort, whereas the physician wants to dispense treatment. The trouble now is that the physician is rich in competence but poor in compassion.

The moral: so long as physicians and patients—and legislators, journalists, and plain ordinary people—persist in confusing the two main justifications of medical treatment, namely, the existence of disease and the expectation of cure, the delivery of even the most technically competent medical care will remain personally unsatisfactory for both patient and physician.

*   *   *

Formerly, when people believed that the human body belonged to God, they concluded that physicians should be allowed to do nothing to it. Nowadays, when people disbelieve that the human body belongs to God, they conclude that there is nothing physicians shouldn't be allowed to do to it.

The religious fundamentalist brooks no limits in his adoration of God, conjuring up an all-powerful deity with whose works man is forbidden to tamper. Created by and in the image of God, man is an infinitely valuable masterpiece which the visitors to the Divine Gallery must not touch, much less alter.

Similarly, the medical fundamentalist brooks no limits in his adoration of Science, conjuring up an all-powerful Medicine capable of endless improvements on all things biological and especially man. Created by and in the image of Medicine, man is an experimental model in the biological technician's laboratory, which it is the duty of every scentist working there to improve.

Clearly, these two world views stand in the same relation to each other as do the negative and positive images of a photograph of the same scene. In each case— whether because of his concept of God or because of his concept of Medicine—man becomes the victim of his own arrogance and intemperance.

* * *

Medicine approaches man as the atheist approaches the Holy Sacrament: as the Host is bread and wine, so man is the structure and function of the human body.

Psychiatry (Psychoanalysis) approaches man as the devout Catholic approaches the Holy Sacrament: as the Host is the body and blood of Christ, so man is the meaning and subjectivity of his own life.

Psychosomatic Medicine approaches man as the Reformed Churches approach the Host: as the Host is both bread and wine and the body and blood of Christ, so man is both matter and meaning, object and subject.

In short, the Christian doctrines of transubstantiation and consubstantiation and their denial are faithfully reproduced in the "scientific" doctrines of Psychiatry, Psychosomatic Medicine, and Medicine.

*   *   *

Formerly, in America, when our religion was Christianity, we fasted and feasted; now that it is Medicine, we diet and go on binges of overeating. Thus was gluttony replaced by obesity, prayer by psychotherapy, the rosary by amphetamines, monasteries by health spas, the clergyman by the clinician, the Vatican by the Food and Drug Administration, and God for whom being slim meant being virtuous by Medical Science for which being slim means being healthy.

*   *   *

Some people believe that a person should have a right to kill himself; that is, that the intention, or alleged intention, to commit suicide should not be punishable by either the criminal or the mental hygiene law.

Others believe that a person should have a right to euthanasia; that is, that, under certain circumstances, a physician should be able to kill a person, unrestrained by the criminal law.

While I support the right to suicide but not the right to euthanasia, it seems to me that there is a right that is prior, that is much more fundamental, than either of these—namely, the right to self-medication, especially of persons suffering from fatal or incurable diseases. In short, I believe that the right of a patient with terminal cancer to take Laetrile or any other "quack medicine" is more elementary than his rights to suicide and euthanasia. Yet, for obvious reasons, this is the right which physicians and the medical profession are the most eager to deny to the patients.

*   *   *

Frequently nowadays individuals go to doctors—especially to general practitioners, family physicians, neurologists, and psychiatrists—for one purpose and one purpose only: to obtain a prescription for a drug they

cannot buy without it. Such a patient is like a small child
wanting a cookie but unable to get into the cookie jar:
the cookie jar being the pharmacy, the cookie the "controlled drug," and the parent—doling out the cookies—
the physician.

* * *

We do not define what is an investment according to
whether or not it will make money for the investor; instead we speak of good and bad investments, as prospective or retrospective judgments. Thus, it is foolish to try
to define what is treatment according to whether or not
it will help the patient to recover from his illness; instead we ought to speak of good and bad treatments, as
prospective and retrospective judgments.

* * *

A well person who claims to be sick and who seeks medical care is said to be neurotic (typically, hypo-
chondriacal); whereas a sick person who claims to be
well and rejects medical care is said to be psychotic
(typically, schizophrenic). These judgments are deeply
revealing of the self-interests of physicians: persons
seeking unnecessary medical attention are condemned
slightly, whereas those shunning necessary medical attention are condemned severely. In the medical ethic,
the greatest crime a patient can commit is to reject the
doctor; and the greatest crime the doctor can commit is
to reveal that the patient does not need, and has a right
to reject, medical care.

* * *

The modern "scientific" physician acquires medical competence at the expense of moral stultification: with ever-
increasing zeal he insists on taking seriously the patient's
illness (bodily or "mental") and correspondingly fails to
take seriously the patient as a person. In short, the physi-

cian transforms the sick person into a case and then treats him as if the doctor, the medical profession, or the state owned him.

* * *

When surgeons operate on the brain of a person with brain disease, they call what they do "neurosurgery"; when they operate on the brain of a person without brain disease, they call it "psychosurgery." It's a nice arrangement for neurosurgeons: it allows them to operate regardless of whether their patient has or has not a disease of the brain; and, because the persons without brain diseases but destined for such surgical interventions are often declared to be legally incompetent on account of "mental illness," it also allows them to operate regardless of whether their ostensible patient requests or rejects the operation.

* * *

If you free a person of his obligation to pay for his treatment, you also deprive him of his right to define what constitutes treatment. Collectivistic planners for "health care," acting in defiance of the proverbial rule that "he who pays the piper may call the tune," may sow the wind of medical idealism, but will reap the whirlwind of medical bestiality.

* * *

When social relations are based on contract, people can obtain many of the things they want in exchange for money. When they are based on commands, they can obtain few, if any, of the things they want in exchange for money; they will therefore try to acquire them in other ways. Drugs and health care in general were formerly obtainable in the free market. For example, a hundred years ago, a person could buy cheaply all the opium, which was pure and safe, that he wanted; today, a person can get opiates legally only if he has a fatal and fearfully painful illness. In other words, we have transferred opiates from the free marketplace to the realm of prizes: some people get Olympic medals; others get shots of morphine. Winners get genuine prizes; losers get consolation prizes. Legal opiates are thus truly the consolation prizes our society gives to those distinguished by dying a painful death.

*   *   *

Today everyone claims to be working for the patient's best interests. No wonder the patient is in deep trouble.

Medicine and Psychiatry

For curing sick bodies, the first requirement is that the sufferer be a patient; whereas for curing sick souls, it is that the healer be patient.

* * *

Doctors control diseases, not persons; psychiatrists control persons, not diseases.

* * *

Physicians, surgeons, and so-called paramedical people are like mechanics, who repair cars, trains, and airplanes. As mechanics do not tell people how or where to travel, medical men should not tell people how or where they ought to live.

Psychiatrists are like travel agents and judges disguised as mechanics, who pretend to work on peoples' cars, while actually counseling or coercing them concerning how and where they ought to live.

* * *

Physicians stubbornly believe that there are two types of pains, organic and psychogenic. The organic, they insist, is caused by a lesion in the body; the psychogenic, by one in the mind. In fact, physicians do not experience, and cannot properly classify, other people's pains. What they experience and classify are other people's complaints. Those complaints of pain which they consider legitimate, doctors call "organic" pains; and those which they consider illegitimate, they call "psychogenic" pains.

It is erroneous to believe, therefore, that organic pain is one kind of pain, and psychogenic pain is another kind, the one standing in the same sort of logical relation to the other as, say, angina pectoris stands to biliary colic. Instead, organic pain is a legitimate complaint and psychogenic pain is an illegitimate complaint, the one standing in the same sort of relation to the other as, for example, real money stands to counterfeit money.

* * *

Because the mind or a person's mental state influences his bodily health, physicians speak of "psychosomatic medicine," and psychiatrists use this term to authenticate themselves as real doctors. But money or a person's economic state also influences his bodily health. Nevertheless, physicians do not speak of "economicosomatic medicine," and economists do not use it to prove that they are real doctors.

* * *

Formerly, when the pathologist was the supreme medical personage, patients were regarded as the carriers of diseased organs or tissues to be preserved in alcohol. Now that the psychopathologist has displaced him, patients are regarded as the carriers of diseased deeds and dispositions to be preserved in archives.

* * *

Psychosurgery changes the way a person thinks, just as plastic surgery changes the way he or she looks. The most important difference between them is that in plastic surgery the intervention is initiated by the person who seeks a change in his or her own body, whereas in psychosurgery it is initiated by a person who seeks a change in someone else's brain. Involuntary lobotomy for schizophrenia might thus be compared to, say, involuntary mastectomy for women with alluring breasts—an intervention that could be justified if those opposed to women having such breasts seized power, decreed the condition a mental disease, and defined mastectomy as the treatment for it.

* * *

Medical pioneers discover new treatments, and formulate new theories of the effects of their treatments, in order to help persons afflicted with certain pre-existing bodily afflictions called "diseases." Banting discovered insulin, Minot discovered liver extract, and Fleming discovered penicillin. Because these substances proved useful for patients suffering from diabetes, pernicious anemia, and certain infectious diseases, they were defined—by physicians, patients, and people generally—as therapeutic agents.

Psychiatric pioneers invent new diseases, and formulate new theories of the etiology of these diseases, in order to justify calling certain pre-existing social interventions "treatments." Kraepelin invented dementia praecox to justify his calling psychiatric imprisonment "mental hospitalization" and regarding it as a form of medical treatment; then, having a new disease on his hands, he attributed it to an as yet undetected defect of the brain. Freud invented the neuroses to justify his calling conversation and confession "psychoanalysis" and regarding it, too, as a form of medical treatment; then, having a class of new diseases on his hands, he attributed them to the "vicissitudes of the Oedipus complex." Menninger invented the idea that everyone is mentally ill to justify his calling everything that anyone did to anyone else ostensibly with good intentions "the therapeutic attitude"; then, having all of life on his hands as a new disease, he attributed it to disturbances in "the vital balance."

In short, real medicine helps real physicians to treat or cure real patients; fake medicine (psychiatry) helps fake physicians (psychiatrists) to influence or control fake patients (the mentally sick).

*   *   *

In medicine, diseases—such as injuries and infections—have always been present and were obviously real, often causing death. For a long time, the treatments of such diseases were magical or metaphorical—such as prayer or the use of extracts from plants and animals to which curative properties were attributed. Conversely, in psychiatry, treatments—such as the use of authority or assaults against the patient with water, drugs, or electricity—have a long history and were obviously real, often causing remission or recovery. It was the diseases for which these treatments were employed that were magical or metaphorical—such as pains and pretendings of various sorts.

Accordingly, the history of medicine is characterized by the earnest search of physicians for treatments to cure the diseases they have on hand and plan to discover; and of psychiatry, by the earnest search of psychiatrists for diseases to justify the treatments they have on hand and plan to develop.

Drugs

Drug abuse conference: people sitting around in smoke-filled rooms discussing the evils of marijuana.

* * *

Experts on drug abuse: merchants in mandated medical mendacities.

* * *

Drug abuseology: the diagnosis and treatment of drug abuse—a branch of psychopathology and psychotherapy; the theory and technique of scapegoating persons labeled as "drug abusers"; the principles and practice of transforming drug into dope, harmless persons into dangerous drug abusers, meddling bureaucrats into medical experts, and tax monies into salaries for the drug abuseologists; in the 1960s and 1970s, the best territory of the medical mafia.

* * *

There are no niggers; there are only black-skinned people whom some white-skinned people don't like and call "niggers." There are no Christ-killers; there are only Jews whom some Christians don't like and call "Christ-killers." Similarly, there are no addicts; there are only people who take some drugs which some other people think they should not take and who therefore call them "addicts."

* * *

Drug abuse is to chemotherapy as heresy is to religion.

* * *

Prescription drugs are to over-the-counter drugs as holy water is to tap water.

Tobacco is to marijuana in America as the Eucharistic wafer is to matzoh in the Catholic Church—or vice versa, in the Jewish temple.

* * *

Methadone maintenance: maintaining the prisoner of pharmacracy on dope and the victimizer on dollars.

* * *

Persons who seek the answer to the so-called drug problem in the prohibition of "dangerous drugs" like to point out that without alcohol there can be no alcoholics and without heroin there can be no heroin addicts. That, of course, is true. But I would like to say to them, and to those who are inclined to listen to them, that prohibiting eating pork or engaging in sex would also prevent trichinosis, impotence, and frigidity. It is in exactly the same way and same sense that an orthodox Jew is protected from trichinosis, a priest from impotence, or a nun from frigidity that the American people seek to protect themselves from drug abuse and drug addiction.

* * *

Question: When is prescribing a drug—officially recognized as a legitimate therapeutic agent, to a consenting patient suffering from an officially recognized illness—not a treatment but a crime? Answer: When the disease is morphine addiction and the therapeutic agent is morphine.

* * *

Question: When does giving drugs to addicts under medical auspices cease to be a crime and become a treatment? Answer: When, like gambling, it is carried out by and under the auspices of the state, rather than by and under the direction of the individual; when, in other words, a heroin addict is given methadone in a clinic under the auspices of an officially sanctioned "maintenance program."

* * *

There is no more reason or justification to restrict the sale of drugs to state-licensed pharmacists than there is to restrict the sale of foods to state-licensed nutritionists.

* * *

We speak of alcoholism, regard it as a medical or mental disease, and try to cure it. But we do not speak of nicotinism and do not regard habitual smoking as a medical or mental disease; indeed, we encourage smoking and acquiesce in the arrogant assaults of smokers on the comfort and health of nonsmokers.

* * *

When formerly in Spain Judaism was prohibited and Catholicism promoted, many Jews became Catholics. We call this "forced religious conversion." When today in the United States heroin is prohibited and methadone promoted, many heroin users become methadone users. We call this "treatment for addiction."

* * *

Traditionally, "temperance" was a trait which a person displayed if he practiced in moderation a habit, such as drinking, which when carried to excess was considered harmful. Toward the end of the nineteenth century, with the birth and rapid growth of the temperance movement, "temperance" came to mean total abstinence from the disapproved habit or substance. Then, around the turn of the century, the term changed not only its meaning but its referent: no longer does "temperance" refer to the speaker's own habits; it now refers to the habits of others which he wants to control, by unbridled force if necessary. Nor, anymore, does it mean moderation; it now means the intemperate prohibition of those habits and substances which the speaker professing "temperance" dislikes and the intemperate persecution of those who disagree with him.

*   *   *

Americans are free to buy guns and bullets, but are not free to buy syringes and drugs. This suggests that Americans are more afraid of injecting themselves with a drug than of being shot by an assailant with a bullet; more afraid of metaphorically shooting themselves than of being literally shot by someone else; in short, that they are more afraid of themselves than of their enemies.

*   *   *

Formerly, had Americans demanded that farmers in a foreign country grow or not grow certain crops, it would have been called colonialism and would have been vigorously opposed by patriots abroad and liberals at home. Now when they demand just this, it is called narcotics control, and is enthusiastically supported by patriots abroad and both liberals and conservatives at home.

For dishonored and dishonorable religious and military colonialisms we have thus cleverly substituted an honored and honorable medical colonialism. Because the latter is ostensibly based on Science and seeks only Health, and because the colonized worship these deities of medical scientism as ardently as do the colonizers, the former are powerless to resist the latter.

* * *

If someone wants to pin a nasty label on you and wants to justify this by what drug you take, there is no use telling him that you are not taking it: he will pin the label on you and say that you are lying. There is also no use telling him that the drug you are taking is harmless: he will pin the label on you and say that you are misguiding the young. Worst of all, there is no use telling him that it's none of his business what you take: he will pin the label on you and say that you are a menace to civilized society. In short, what you have to tell a person who wants to stigmatize you because of what you take is not that the *drug is harmless* (assuming that it is)—but that *he is harmful*. To be able to do that successfully, you must have more prestige or power or both than your would-be stigmatizer has. When the stigmatizer can identify himself with the full force of conventional wisdom and popular sentiment, the person to be stigmatized can ill afford to resist on moral or ideological grounds: the more "innocent" he is or the more valid are his arguments, the more necessary it will be for his opponents to deface and invalidate him.

* * *

The undesirable or pathological effects of psychoactive drugs administered by physicians to patients are called "drug reactions" and are treated by anesthesiologists, internists, and other medical specialists. The identical effects of these drugs administered by individuals to themselves are called "bad trips" and are treated by psychiatrists. This is as if gunshot wounds of the head inflicted on individuals by assailants were called one thing and treated by neurosurgeons, while those inflicted on individuals by themselves were called another and treated by psychiatrists.

* * *

Ostensibly, the use of illicit drugs, like marijuana and heroin, is prohibited because they are said to impair the social functioning of the person who uses them. This claim is inconsistent with the fact that the authorities concerned—mainly parents, politicians, and physicians—usually don't know who uses such drugs; and that they support costly efforts to develop and deploy tests to detect illicit drug users. (Many such tests, moreover, are carried out without the subject's knowledge of being tested or without his consent to it.)

If illicit drugs impair social functioning—a contingency which is clearly absurd without specifying drugs and dosages—then we need no special tests to identify the users. And if they do not necessarily impair social functioning—which is clearly the case—then testing people for drug abuse by examining their urines is unlike testing them for diabetes and is instead more like testing men for Jewishness by examining their penises.

* * *

Those who sell illicit drugs offer drugs to people and money to policemen.

In relation to the number of customers to which each of these commodities is offered, money is probably a more powerful lure than heroin; nevertheless, tempting with drugs is called "pushing dope," while tempting with money is called simply "offering a bribe."

* * *

Legitimate entrepreneurs, whom we call businessmen, must advertise and sell their product in an open, competitive market. Illegitimate entrepreneurs, whom we call "pushers" if they sell drugs, have their advertising done for them by the government, by what we call "drug abuse education"; and they sell their product in a closed, noncompetitive market.

The current American drug scene thus epitomizes communist economics and psychology: inferior products sold at exorbitant prices; masses of dissatisfied, if not actually poisoned, customers at the mercy of a handful of "profiteering" producers and distributors; and the government waging tacit war on consumers and open war on producers—thus fulfilling its essential political function, to rule over the ruled.

* * *

In Jewish history, at first anyone could offer God a sacrifice, then only the rabbi could, and finally no one could—the ritual sacrifice being replaced with the ritual study of sacrifice. In Western medical history, there is a similar progression with respect to certain drugs we now call "dangerous" (typically opium and certain opiates): at first, anyone could give or take such drugs; then only physicians could give them and only patients could take them; finally, no one could do either—the use and avoidance of these substances being replaced with propaganda about their use and avoidance.

* * *

Pharmacology is the science of drug use, that is, of the healing (therapeutic) and harming (toxic) effects of drugs. Nevertheless, all textbooks of pharmacology contain a chapter on drug abuse and drug addiction—and no one finds anything strange or objectionable in this. But, by the same token, textbooks of anatomy should contain a chapter on the inferiority of women or of alien races; textbooks of gynecology and urology, a chapter on promiscuity and prostitution; textbooks of physiology, a chapter on perversions; and, of course, textbooks on astronomy, a chapter on sun worship. In short, not until we distinguish more clearly than we now do between the chemical and ceremonial uses and effects of drugs shall we be able to begin a reasonable discussion and a sensible description of what we now call "drug abuse" and "drug addiction."

* * *

If society wishes to encourage the relief of pain, both literal and metaphorical, through medication by doctors and to discourage its relief through self-medication, it will glorify the medical profession and the drugs physicians prescribe and will vilify "pushers" and self-medication—which it will call "drug abuse."

Likewise, if society wishes to encourage the relief of sexual needs, both literal and metaphorical, through marriage and to discourage their relief through masturbation, it will glorify marriage and the sexual pleasures partners bestow on each other and will vilify "pornographers" and sexual self-satisfaction—which it will call "self-abuse."

In short, pornography stands in the same relation to masturbation as narcotic and soporific drugs stand to medicine. Should society invert its traditional rank ordering of these values, as some Scandinavian countries have recently done with respect to sex, it will consider pornography "beneficial" and will not only permit it but encourage it. Accordingly, only when society will rank self-medication over medication by doctors, will it consider so-called dangerous drugs "beneficial," which it will then not only "legalize" but "push."

* * *

A hundred years ago, a person could obtain in the free market all the pure and safe opium he wanted in exchange for a very small amount of money. Today, he can obtain a small quantity of impure and unsafe opium on the black market for a very large amount of money and the risk of going to jail for life for buying it; and he can obtain minute quantities of opiates from a physician for incurable cancer and appropriate complaints of pain. This, despite our vast advances in medical science and technology, is where the anticapitalist mentality in medicine has brought us: we get steadily better at curing sickness and worse at comforting the sick.

Suicide

In growing up, children learn to what extent they are expected and allowed to take their own lives in their hands. The more they are and the more they do so, the more fully do they develop into autonomous, self-determining persons—who not only take their own lives in their hands, but who also take their own lives. This is why those who choose to be their own masters often also choose to be their own executioners.

*　*　*

If a person doesn't know what to do with his life, he may save it for future use or decide that it's of no use and throw it away. We regard throwing away useless junk as a quite reasonable thing to do; but we regard throwing away a useless life as a symptom of mental illness.

*　*　*

Today, if a priest claimed that non-Christians, although they do not say so, want to be rescued from ignorance and be converted to Christianity, his claim would be dismissed as self-serving; that is, it would be viewed as an assertion not about his subjects' wanting to be saved, but about his wanting to save them.

However, when a psychiatrist now claims that those attempting suicide, although they do not say so, want to be rescued from death and be helped to live a happy and healthy life, his claim is accepted as a scientific statement; that is, it is viewed as an assertion about his subjects' desire to be rescued, rather than about his own desire to rescue them.

*   *   *

In language and logic we are the prisoners of our premises, just as in politics and law we are the prisoners of our rulers. Hence we had better pick them well. For if suicide is an illness because it terminates in death and if the prevention of death by any means necessary is the physician's therapeutic mandate, then the proper remedy for suicide is indeed liberticide.

Psychiatry

The subject matter of psychiatry is neither minds nor mental diseases, but lies—the "patient's" and the "psychiatrist's." These lies begin with the names of the participants in the transaction—the designation of one party as "patient" even though he is not ill and of the other as "therapist" even though he is not treating any illness. They continue with the lies that comprise the subject matter proper of the discipline—the psychiatric "diagnoses," "prognoses," "treatments," and "follow-ups." And they end with the lies that, like shadows, follow ex-mental patients through the rest of their lives—the records of denigrations called "depression," "schizophrenia," or whatnot and of imprisonments called "hospitalization."

Accordingly, if we wished to give psychiatry an honest name, we could call it "mendacitology," or the study of lies.

* * *

The very existence of disciplines like psychiatry and abnormal psychology authenticates the "reality" of mental diseases and disorders.

Many disciplines deal with the study of human behavior without, however, splitting themselves into normal and abnormal, healthy and sick, subdivisions. There is no "developmental economics" dealing with booms and "abnormal economics" dealing with busts; no "developmental political science" dealing with peace, and "abnormal political science" dealing with war. But there is a "developmental psychology" dealing with conforming behavior and "abnormal psychology" dealing with deviant behavior, and a "psychiatry" dealing with diseased behavior.

*   *   *

The principal subject matter of psychiatry is disagreement—usually disagreement between two persons, sometimes disagreement between an individual and a group. The simplest way to resolve disagreement is by one of the parties capitulating to the other.

In institutional psychiatry, disagreement is resolved by the psychiatrist coercing the patient. This is like the traditional imperialist or colonialist posture—a superior power crudely dominating an inferior one.

In antipsychiatry, disagreement is resolved by the psychiatrist capitulating to the patient. This is like the modern pacifist, foreign-aid-from-guilt posture: a superior power abjectly appeasing an inferior one.

While in his personal life, the psychiatrist cannot avoid or evade disagreement and conflict any more than any other person can, as a psychiatrist, he can try to arrange his life in such a way that his relationships with his clients are co-operative rather than antagonistic. The simplest way to accomplish this is by not entering into a relationship with an involuntary client and by refusing both to dominate clients or to be dominated by them.

*   *   *

Psychiatrists may be classified, according to what they do, as follows:

I. Those in the housing and real-estate business.

1. Psychiatrists in public mental hospitals: operators of flophouses and cheap hotels and wardens to the poor and unimportant and their unwanted relatives.

2. Psychiatrists in private mental hospitals: resort operators, hotelkeepers, and wardens to the rich and important and their unwanted relatives.

3. Antipsychiatrists in "communities" and "counterinstitutions": operators of flophouses and cheap hotels for the poor and unimportant.

II. Those in the drug business.

1. Neuropharmacological psychiatrists: dealers in psychopharmacologicals.

2. General psychiatrists: dealers in a combination of psychopharmacologicals and advice regarding life-management.

III. Those in the brain-damage business.

1. The electroshockers: dealers in artificial epilepsy.

2. The insulin-coma producers: dealers in insulin overdosage.

IV. Those in the conversation business.

1. Psychoanalysts: dealers in the cult of Freudianism.

2. Dynamic psychotherapists: dealers in adjustment to the dominant ethic.

3. Psychotherapists of other persuasions: dealers in the principles and practices of various ethical systems.

* * *

Psychiatric diagnosis: medical mugging.

* * *

Psychiatric diagnostician: licensed libeler.

* * *

Psychiatric logic: if a person takes a drug prescribed for him by a physician and claims that it makes him feel better, that proves that mental illness is a bona-fide disease; but if a person takes a drug prohibited for him by physicians and legislators and claims that it makes him feel better, that proves that he is an addict.

*   *   *

Psychiatric nosology: a dictionary of defamations disguised as diagnoses.

*   *   *

Psychopathology: calling problems in living "diseases."

Psychotherapy: calling the psychiatric mystification of problems in living "treatments."

Psychohistory: calling the vilification of hated and the glorification of loved historical figures the "product of impartial psychiatric-historical research."

*   *   *

Psychohistorian: a person, envious and cowardly, who, unable to defeat his adversary in open combat, defames him with a diagnosis; who, unable to bring him to his knees, brings him to his neurosis; who, in short, pretends to describe great men and women, when, in fact, he despoils them. The psychohistorians are thus the Clifford Irvings of historiography: since they don't know their subjects, they invent them; and since they usually don't like their subjects and write about them only to aggrandize themselves, the people they invent are usually mean and ugly.

*   *   *

Postpartum depression: the hangover after the honeymoon.

*   *   *

Legal insanity: the disease whose etiology is being caught

committing a crime, and whose precipitating cause is being indicted for it.

* * *

The insanity plea: a psychiatric alibi based on the scientificization of Christianity; evil deeds formerly attributed to the devil who possessed the defendant are transformed into "irresistible impulses" which make him insane. In either case, the defendant claims that he did not carry out his criminal act himself, but that it was performed "through his body" by the devil or by his irresistible impulse. In short, when people believed in the devil, they believed that diabolical possession caused crime; when people believe in insanity, they believe that mental illness causes crime.

* * *

Psychosomatic medicine: the "philosophy" according to which bodily diseases are mental and mental diseases, physical. This nonsense satisfies the dual aims of professionalism—exalting the expert by claiming that everything is something other than what it seems and debasing the layman by confounding common sense.

* * *

Psychiatric theory: either an assertion of the obvious couched in technical jargon or a false generalization of personal conduct as psychological law.

* * *

The logic of therapeutic empiricism in psychiatry: A man lights up in the nonsmoking compartment of a train. His fellow passenger starts coughing. Blue in the face, the nonsmoker says: "I wish you wouldn't smoke. You know, it's not healthy." The smoker replies: "You are mistaken. I smoke and don't cough. You don't smoke and cough."

* * *

The manic person acts as if everything in the world were of the utmost concern and interest to him; the depressed person, as if nothing were. The former tries to cover up the fact that he is bored by his own life; the latter, that he is disgusted by it.

* * *

As an old psychiatric joke has it, the neurotic builds castles in the air, the psychotic lives in them, and the psychiatrist collects the rent. I would add that the psychiatrist builds a profession and prisons on a metaphor, the neurotic seeks solace in them, and the psychotic is sentenced to them.

* * *

Human beings exist in two states of consciousness: asleep and awake. Psychiatry may be used to make persons either more asleep or more awake. Thus, both chemotherapy and psychotherapy may either sedate or stimulate the patient—depending on the nature of the drug he ingests and on the nature of the conversation in which he engages.

* * *

People often seek psychiatric help—from psychotherapy to mental hospitalization—because they feel that they wish they were dead; when their "therapy" is completed, they often are dead but do not mind it.

* * *

Husbands and wives at odds with each other often attribute that part of their partner's behavior which offends them to one of two causes: if the partner is not "in therapy" and "refuses to seek help," then to "mental illness"; and if he is in therapy, then to his "treatment." In each case, the person who so treats his partner illegitimizes his partner's motives and demeans him as a person—which is often the original reason for their being at odds with one another.

* * *

Psychiatry is the sewer into which societies in the second half of the twentieth century discharge all their unsolved moral and social problems. As sewers emptying into rivers or oceans pollute the waters into which they discharge, so psychiatry emptying into medicine pollutes the care and cure of the sick.

* * *

Psychiatrists are trained in medicine which they don't practice and practice psychotherapy in which they are not trained.

* * *

Psychiatry: Dr. Jones doesn't like what Mr. Smith does and calls him mentally ill.

Antipsychiatry: Mr. Smith doesn't like what Dr. Jones does and calls him mentally ill.

My position: Dr. Jones and Mr. Smith don't like each other. To be sure, declaring that one does not like someone is much weaker than diagnosing someone as mentally sick. If we describe our adversary, in plain English, as our enemy, we continue to recognize him as fully human; but if we diagnose him, in the defamatory rhetoric of psychiatry or antipsychiatry, as mad, then we no longer recognize him as fully human. Herein lies the appeal of the madness-mongering imagery and language of both psychiatry and antipsychiatry: each renders the speaker effortlessly superior to his adversary.

* * *

It is one thing to oppose clerical coercion and theocratic tyranny as, for example, Jefferson and Emerson did; it is quite another to oppose religious beliefs and observances as, for example, Freud and Lenin did. Similarly, it is one thing to oppose clinical coercion and psychiatric oppression, as I do; and it is quite another to oppose psychiatric convictions and contracts, as the antipsychiatrists do. In short, those who advocate freedom from religious or psychiatric oppression object not to religion or psychiatry, but to oppression; whereas those who advocate anticlericalism or antipsychiatry, object not to oppression but to priests and psychiatrists.

* * *

Nearly everyone who speaks of the "medical model" in psychiatry uses this term incorrectly. Those who support the "medical model" evidently believe that if they could convince the politicians that "mental patients" are sick, they could treat them for their illness, regardless of whether or not the patients want to be treated. Hence, they act not like internists but like pediatricians, who must convince the parents that their child is sick and, having convinced them, can treat the child, regardless of whether or not he wants to be treated.

Those who oppose the "medical model" evidently believe that if they could convince the politicians that "mental patients" are not sick, they could prevent physicians from treating them as if they were ill, regardless of whether or not the patients want to be treated. Hence, they, too, act like pediatricians, who, if they can convince the parents that their child is not sick, can prevent the child from being treated, regardless of whether or not he wants to be treated.

All this illustrates that both institutional psychiatry and antipsychiatry rest on the "pediatric model" characterized by domination and coercion—rather than on a truly "medical model" characterized by co-operation and contract.

* * *

In every field of clinical medicine except psychiatry,

physicians gain their reputation from their skill in treating patients. Influential and prominent psychiatrists—who claim the most insistently that psychiatry is a medical specialty like any other—acquire their prominence not for what they do for their patients, but for what they do for their colleagues. This is consistent with the fact that in psychiatry, unlike other fields of medical practice, physicians are "made great" by their followers, not their patients. Hence, those psychiatrists who command the greatest surplus of private patients for referral to loyal followers, and who control the largest public or private grants for "mental health care" for dispensing to loyal followers, together with the power and willingness to withdraw all economic and ideological supports from followers at the least sign of independence, will acquire the greatest number of disciples, who will, in turn, define their benefactor as a "great psychiatrist." In short, economic and ideological power over colleagues, not therapeutic skill, is the ground on which the fame of many prominent psychiatrists rests. Psychiatric leaders—from Bleuler and Freud to Alexander, Menninger, and Grinker—are thus more like mafioso godfathers than like prominent medical practitioners: each controls a certain territory for those under his "protection," who, in turn, "protect" him by economic and ideological tithing and by unceasing hostility against, and readiness to do battle with, other psychiatric godfathers.

* * *

Because psychiatry is, and has always been, a major ideology and institution, it has supplied certain identities and jobs to various individuals and groups.

The asylum keepers, from Pinel to Bleuler and beyond, gave some persons the identity of madmen and the job of menial labor in the madhouse; to others, they gave the identity of madhouse keepers and the job of caring for madmen.

Freud and the psychoanalytic pioneers created two similar sets of identities and employments: to some, they gave the job of professional psychoanalytic patient, exemplified by the Russian aristocrat who fell on hard times and became known as the "Wolf Man"; to others, the job of professional psychoanalyst, exemplified by the many laymen-patients who became therapists.

Inevitably, I, too, have generated new identities and jobs; for some, as ex-patients combating psychiatric oppression, exemplified by the various patient liberation groups; for others, as attorneys litigating for the rights of mental patients, suing psychiatrists for malpractice, and otherwise harassing mad-doctors and the madness establishment.

* * *

Civil liberties stand in approximately the same relation to the practice of psychiatry as physiological processes stand to the practice of medicine. However, while prospective and practicing physicians study and pay attention to physiology, prospective and practicing psychiatrists neither study nor pay attention to civil liberties.

* * *

When women are unhappy after having a baby, psychiatrists categorize their loss of freedom as a disease and say they suffer from "postpartum depression." But when men are unhappy after a stock-market crash, psychiatrists don't categorize their loss of money as a disease and don't say they suffer from "postcrash depression."

* * *

If a person cuts off his own penis and so relieves his own guilt, shame, and anxiety, it's called "self-castration" which is considered to be an illness; if he hires someone to destroy his brain by electricity or surgery and so relieves his guilt, shame, and anxiety, it's called "electroshock" and "lobotomy," which are considered to be treatments.

* * *

If a person "breaks the law," the police will get him. If he "has a break with reality," the psychiatrist will.

* * *

Some people lead lives that are bad jokes; others make bad jokes about them. The former are the psychotics; the latter, the psychiatrists.

* * *

Psychiatrists are fond of calling old patients who are tired of acting psychotic and for whom the hospital ward has become a home "burned-out schizophrenics." They might as well call old doctors who are tired of acting psychiatric or psychoanalytic and for whom the hospital office or analytic institute has become a home "burned-out psychiatrists" or "burned-out psychoanalysts."

* * *

The more unacceptable the metaphor in which the so-called psychiatric patient couches his complaints, the more "bizarre" is said to be his "symptom" and the more "serious" his "disease." Thus, if the "patient" complains about his life in the metaphors of medicine, the psychiatrist says he suffers from hysteria or hypochondriasis; while if he complains in the metaphors of religion, the psychiatrist says he suffers from paranoia or schizophrenia.

* * *

In everyday life, if Jones does not understand what Smith tells him, Jones is considered to be stupid; but in psychiatry, if Jones is a psychiatrist and Smith a patient and if Jones does not understand what Smith tells him, then Smith is considered to be crazy.

* * *

Trying to prove that they are real doctors, psychiatrists speak in the language of medical jargon. Thus, they refer to the things they do as "treatments" and use the standard martial metaphors of modern medicine: claiming to possess a "therapeutic armamentarium," they preach the importance of choosing the right "weapons" from it with which to combat the "diseases" which "attack," "incapacitate," and "kill" their "patients."

This imagery is not so bad for describing ordinary medical treatments, where physician and patient may be pictured as joining in a therapeutic alliance combatting, with the "weapons" of modern medicine, the illness. But this same imagery becomes a trap in psychiatry, where there is no illness in the ordinary sense, where the illness is itself a metaphor, and, hence, where there are only two targets in the field against which the psychiatrist can turn his weapons: his "patient" and himself. When, as is usually the case, the psychiatrist "attacks" the patient, the result is the butchery that has been called, and is still called, "psychiatric treatment"; and when, as is sometimes the case, the psychiatrist "attacks" himself, the result is a self-butchery, manifested by his moral degradation and physical self-destruction.

* * *

Reflections on the *DSM-II*, otherwise known as the American Psychiatric Association's *Diagnostic and Statistical Manual of Mental Disorders*.

Under the category "302:Sexual Deviations," this *Manual* lists such mental diseases as "302.1:Fetishism," "302.2:Pedophilia," "302.3:Transvestitism," "302.4:Exhibitionism," and "302.5:Voyeurism."

Now that "302.0:Homosexuality" has been removed from the list by a vote of the membership of this association, the association should consider adding to it several conditions recently discovered to be mental diseases. The following seem to me the most likely candidates.

"302.10:Continence," "302.11:Celibacy," "302.12:Pornophilia" (excessive love of prostitutes or of a "swinging" life style), "302.13:Pornophobia" (morbid fear of prostitutes or of a "swinging" life style), "302.14:Pornographomania" (morbid interest in pornography), "302.15:Nudismophobia" (fear of being seen nude).

These diseases are only the most obvious manifestations of a veritable plague of sexual dysfunctions discovered during the past few years by the brilliant investigations of modern sexologists.

* * *

From the Question-and-Answer department of the journal *The Medical Aspects of Human Sexuality:*

"Q. What is the psychodynamic basis for considering nailbiting as a form of masturbation?

"A. Nailbiting may represent a substitution for masturbation . . ."*

The logic: masturbation may therefore represent a substitution for nailbiting.

The moral: if this be "psychodynamics," let the buyer beware of psychodiagnostics, psychosomatics, psychotherapeutics, and all the other psycho-prefixed pomposities of psychiatry.

* * *

Psychiatry is either a medical specialty devoted to healing the sick—or a monstrous parody of it, concealing bestialities of which no beasts other than human beings are capable. Believing the former, countless people become

---

* "Nailbiting and Masturbation," *The Medical Aspects of Human Sexuality,* November 1974, p. 171.

the willing, albeit somewhat unwitting, victims of it. Many of them are now, at last, turning on their tormentors. I sympathize with them and support their efforts to abolish involuntary psychiatric interventions. But it seems to me that only when enough people have suffered as these people have, will the American people, and people elsewhere, realize that they cannot eat their cake and have it too: that they cannot protect their personal dignity and self-responsibility and, at the same time, promote the systematic destruction of these values through a psychiatric inquisition whose "therapy" they themselves crave and whose terrors they themselves help to create.

*   *   *

The moral depravity and obtuseness of modern psychiatric and psychoanalytic educators is displayed dramatically by their aim: to train young psychiatrists to be dispassionate scientists of the mind, and compassionate healers of the sick mind. But compassion without passion is as impossible as trial without error, joy without sadness.

Actually, psychiatrists try to be, and teach their students to be, dispassionate: the analyst as a mirror in which the analysand can view his own unconscious or the therapist as a surgeon "operating" on the "wound" of the patient's problems are favorite psychiatric metaphors for the proper psychiatric posture. But in proportion, as the psychiatrist succeeds in becoming dispassionate toward the moral tragedies of life, as it is lived in his own society by his own patients, he also becomes incapable of being compassionate. It is in this sense, and for this reason, that psychiatric training actually incapacitates the trainee for rendering decent and dignified help to people with their problems in living.

Freud was, of course, a passionate person. But instead

of using his passion to fuel his compassion, he used it to energize his advocacy for his own "cause" and religion—namely, psychoanalysis. Jung, Adler, and many of Freud's followers who left him and who were also passionate persons, faced, sooner or later, this conflict of whether to channel their passion toward caring for Freud and psychoanalysis or toward caring for the patient and his problems. The condition for becoming and remaining a loyal psychoanalyst was to opt for submission to Freud rather than respect for the patient, for adherence to psychoanalysis rather than efforts to relieve suffering.

* * *

Not only is the metaphor of health misused in psychiatry, but so too is the metaphor of growth. Psychiatrists, and so-called mental health professionals generally, are fond of speaking of the "growth, development, and maturity of the personality." However, the whole point of being a person is being able and free to make choices and to be responsible for their consequences. An acorn does not choose to become an oak tree; but a young person does choose to become a doctor or a dentist, a priest or a politician—a tolerant or tyrannical adult.

* * *

The aim of physical theory is to enhance our understanding of the world; the aim of psychological theory is to enhance the self-esteem of the psychologist.

* * *

One of the major dilemmas of psychiatry—as the study and influencing of problematic behavior—is that one often doesn't know what is a problem and what is a solution to a problem. In fact, each problem is the solution to some other problems, and each solution is another problem requiring solution.

* * *

If madness is monologue or dialogue, then there are only two ways of altering it. First, we can help the speaker to change himself; he will then become a different person who will say different things in different ways. Second, we can change the language or, more precisely, damage or destroy it; the "patient" will then no longer be able to express himself in the mad ways he had been accustomed to using.

The former method is undramatic and works best when it is spontaneous; and it looks "ineffective" because it is never clear what the professional has done for the client and what the client has done for himself. The second method (for example, drugs, electroshock, lobotomy) is dramatic and has the appearance of being extremely effective (or destructive, depending on one's point of view) because the professional does indeed affect the client in a very powerful fashion.

* * *

Some of my critics dismiss my writings on psychiatry with the complaint that I pay too much attention to economics and the declaration that I am unfamiliar with and ignore the "masses of poor people" who are cared for in the public clinics and hospitals.

In my view, the first half of this claim is valid and the second is not. In fact, I have stated my views on psychiatry and the poor clearly enough and would summarize them as follows. Poor people, by definition, have no money and hence cannot pay, in real currency, for what they want. They therefore pay for it in the only currency they have, namely, pain, suffering, and the willingness to submit to medical and psychiatric authorities. And what is it that they want and so obtain? Personal attention disguised as medical and psychiatric care; sedatives and stimulants disguised as treatments; and, finally, room and board disguised as hospitalization.

* * *

The fundamental error of psychiatry is that it regards life as a problem to be solved, instead of as a purpose to be fulfilled.

Institutional Psychiatry

Institutional psychiatry is like monetary inflation: as the latter is created by fiat money, that is, by slapping ink on paper and then calling it "currency," so the former is created by fiat slander, that is, by slapping insults on people and then calling them "patients."

* * *

Institutional psychiatry offers solutions to problems of housing by camouflaging them as problems of health: it defines those who are homeless or who cannot get along with others under the same roof as "mentally ill"; confines those so defined in madhouses called "hospitals"; and justifies this enterprise in forcible eviction and relocation as a form of "medical treatment."

* * *

Institutional psychiatrists who work in mental hospitals are well-paid wardens; antipsychiatrists who work in "antihospitals" are poorly paid slumlords.

* * *

Right to treatment: according to both the American Civil Liberties Union and the American Psychiatric Association, the "constitutional right" of an involuntary

mental patient to psychiatric treatment; actually, the institutional psychiatrist's right to torture his victim and
call it "treatment." In short, the patient's "right to treatment" is a euphemism for the psychiatrist's "right to
treat," whether the patient likes it or not.

* * *

Marriage without a marriage certificate would not be
marriage at all. Similarly, madness without a madness
certificate—that is, without the certification of the patient
as psychotic, and of his protector-punisher as his
psychiatrist—would not be madness at all. This is why I
believe that just as there could be no meaningful protection of wives against husbands, or vice versa, so long as
women were not completely free to sever the bonds of
matrimony that tied them to their husbands, so there can
be no meaningful protection of mental patients against
institutional psychiatrists so long as persons accused of
mental illness are not completely free to sever the bonds
that tie them to their psychiatrists.

* * *

As mating is both the cause and consequence of holy
matrimony or the wife-husband relationship, so madness
is both the cause and consequence of psychiatric matrimony or the psychotic-psychiatrist relationship.

As, in some societies, mating outside of matrimony is
prohibited and is called "fornication," so in others,
madness outside of the madhouse is prohibited and is
called "dangerousness to self and others." The fact that
both "fornication" and "dangerousness to self and
others" actually flourish outside of the protective walls of
these institutions serves only to strengthen the illusory
protections which marriage and the madhouse provide
against the inexorable uncertainties and vicissitudes of
life.

* * *

Most persons now said to be chronically mentally ill, many of whom go to or stay in mental hospitals voluntarily, are individuals who have refused to make a commitment either to living or to dying. The result is that they become embalmed, as it were—half-alive and half-dead—and often remain, perhaps for this reason, in amazingly good physical health and "live" for a long time.

* * *

The latest obscenity in the history of institutional psychiatry is the forcible de-institutionalization of the chronic mental patient for whom the hospital has become a home. In the United States today, individuals who want to stay out of mental hospitals are still "admitted" to them against their will; whereas individuals who want to stay in such hospitals are "discharged" from them against their will in ever increasing numbers. The result is that while the prison function of the mental hospital remains unchanged, its asylum function is progressively eroded.

* * *

When psychiatrists go to court in an effort to prove that a person is mentally ill and dangerous to himself or others—a process known as a "commitment" hearing or trial—and win their case, it proves that the "patient" is "insane" and that they, the psychiatrists, are great humanitarians. On the other hand, when patients go to court in an effort to prove that a mental hospital superintendent is depriving them of their civil rights—a process now known as a "class-action suit"—and win their case, it still proves, according to the psychiatrists, that the "patients" are "mentally ill" and that they, the institutional managers, are great humanitarians.

By the end of 1973 "approximately thirty class-action suits of major significance [were] under way across the nation—all of them relating to the rights of patients." This is the way Milton Greenblatt, M.D.—who as former

Massachusetts Mental Health Commissioner had been a
defendant in one of these suits—sees this development:
"In a sense, we were the scapegoats for what society
had failed to do for its unfortunates. Although in truth,
we had tried hard to depopulate hospitals and [state]
schools, to evolve better alternatives . . . The adminis-
trator of public programs, although battered by winds of
controversy, may nevertheless take pride in his role as
actor in a modern drama."*

Just as to the slaveholder, sincerely believing in the
benefits of slavery for the Negro, the black always
remained a slave or slavelike creature and he, himself, a
noble protector of the weak—so, to the institutional psychiatrist, sincerely believing in the benefits of psychiatric
incarceration for the madman, the mental hospital in-
mate will always remain a mentally diseased or disor-
dered patient and he, himself, a noble physician curing
the sick.

* * *

Not satisfied with the controls of contract, some critics of
psychiatric brutalities seek the remedy in the enemy—the
state—for example, by advocating the prohibition of
lobotomy. However, since they cannot advocate
prohibiting a therapeutic procedure, they, too, must first
rename what they want to remove: they say that lobotomy is not medicine but mutilation.

But who defines "mutilation"? Is abortion not mutilation? Or the ritual circumcision of a healthy infant?

Contract and consent suffice to protect those who
want to be protected. Any attempt to extend protection
beyond this limit makes the "reformers" indistinguisha-
ble from the therapeutic totalitarians they oppose.

* * *

* Quoted in "APA Hoists Test Balloons over Crisis Areas: Fund
Erosion, Class Action Suits," CMHCs, *Roche Report: Frontiers of
Psychiatry,* 3:1–2, 6–8 (Nov. 1), 1973; p. 8.

In the mental hospital, both patient and doctor are alienated from real work—that is, from work which results in a salable product or a service. Deprived of the reward of having been useful to someone, both patient and psychiatrist seek their reward in power. The patient becomes ever more intoxicated with his imaginary power over the creations of his private world—his "psychosis"; the psychiatrist becomes ever more intoxicated with his real power over the creations of his public world—his "psychotic patients." The "deterioration" of the mental hospital patients is paralleled by a similar "deterioration" of the mental hospital psychiatrist: both suffer the consequences of an overweening striving for power over others. Or, as the moralists used to put it, both are punished for being evil.

Psychoanalysis

Psychoanalysis is the trade name of a certain kind of conversation, just as Coca-Cola and Kentucky Fried Chicken are the trade names of a certain kind of cola drink and fried chicken.

Psychoanalysis is also the name of a body of speculations about life and human relations put forward by the originator of that trade name.

*　*　*

Resistance: the patient's reluctance to keep paying his analyst for a service that is of no value to him.

*　*　*

Dissident: one who denies the divinity of Freud; the opposite of "orthodox."

*　*　*

Orthodox: one who recognizes the divinity of Freud; after proven in battle against dissidents, a candidate for a bishopric in one of the training institutes.

*　*　*

The patient is narcissistic, the analyst has self-esteem; the patient is inhibited, the analyst has self-control; the patient is promiscuous, the analyst is liberated; in short, the patient is immature and mentally ill, while the analyst is mature and mentally healthy.

* * *

The term "psychoanalysis" is itself a strategically literalized metaphor—devised and deployed to make it seem as if "psyche" were like blood or urine and could be analyzed as such. Playing this language game for all it's worth, some psychiatrists have duly claimed to have invented "psychosynthesis."

* * *

Freud converted speech into a specimen—to be "analyzed" by means of the fake technique of free association; dreams into dung—the excrement of the mental apparatus in which the analyst as laboratory technician searches for the pathological contents of the patient's unconscious mind; and legendary heroes, like Oedipus, into "complexes"—henceforth to serve as the labels of mankind's innate and incurable insanities. In short, he medicalized, and thus dehumanized, language, history, and the whole of human existence.

* * *

Psychoanalysis now serves as a language for concealing and repressing the existence of moral conflicts and choices, just as formerly Latin served as a language for concealing and repressing the existence of sexual body parts and performances.

* * *

Freud gave the right account of psychoanalysis, but placed it in the wrong category: he described it as a type of contract and conversation, but classified it as a type of treatment. This is one of the reasons for the hopeless confusion and controversy about whether or not psychoanalysis is a type of medical practice: insofar as it is couched in the language of medicine—as a treatment for an illness—it belongs to medicine; and insofar as it is couched in the language of communication and contract —as a conversation about a person's past and present methods of coping with life—it does not belong to medicine.

* * *

Freud was more adept at using psychoanalysis to harm his rivals than to help his patients. He did so, partly, because he was a bitter and nasty man; partly, because it is easier to use psychoanalysis to hurt than to heal; and partly, because the so-called intellectuals are more interested in seeing great men put down by psychoanalytic "diagnoses" than seeing ordinary men raised up by psychoanalytic "treatment."

* * *

Freud and the Freudians have deprived Jung of many of his best ideas and, to boot, have defamed him as an anti-Semite. Actually, Jung was far more candid and correct than Freud in identifying psychotherapy as an ethical rather than technical enterprise; and Freud was far more anti-Christian than Jung was anti-Semitic.

* * *

Sigmund Freud was like Henry Ford: each developed a "better mousetrap"—Freud for lunacy, Ford for locomotion. But in insisting that psychoanalysis was not conversation but a special type of treatment, Freud made a claim as patently false and fraudulent as would Ford's claim have been had he insisted that the Model-T was not a car but a special type of horse. Freud's achievement thus lay not so much in his discovery, which, like Ford's, was not his, but in his ability to make people accept his classification of the car as a horse—of conversation as treatment. Freud was, indeed, a genius—but, in my opinion, an evil genius.

* * *

In Freud's Vienna a male was relieved of his hunger as a baby by a wet nurse; of his bowel contents as a child by enemas; and of his sexual tensions as a young adult, and often later on as well, by prostitutes. On the basis of these experiences, Freud had set himself up as the psychosexual legislator of mankind.

* * *

Psychoanalysis is a new version of Judaism. The Orthodox Jew believes that the Jews are the Chosen People, superior to all others. The Orthodox Psychoanalyst and Psychoanalysand believe that analysts and analyzed patients are the Healthy People, superior to all others.

* * *

The Eucharist stands in the same relation to a snack of bread and wine as psychoanalytic treatment stands to ordinary conversation. The fact that the Host is bread is overshadowed, in the minds of the faithful, by the awe and respect they feel for the Church. Similarly, the fact that psychoanalysis is conversation is overshadowed, in the minds of the faithful, by the awe and respect they feel for medicine.

* * *

The psychoanalyst looks at all forms of behavior as the puritan looks at illicit sex: that is, intellectually, he wants to replace the subject's enjoyment of his own behavior by the authority's explanation of it, and practically, he wants to use his explanation as a justification for condemning, forbidding, or otherwise regulating the subject's behavior. In short, while seemingly psychoanalysis is the sexualization of behavior, actually it is its puritanization.

* * *

The satirist deflates personal pomposities and social hypocrisies by ridiculing them; his medium is laughter, his method is poking fun. The psychoanalyst inflates personal problems and social conventions by crying over them; his medium is tears, his method is making diagnoses.

Satire is thus in the tradition of the Greeks and the Christians, of Aristophanes and Swift. Psychoanalysis is in the tradition of the Jews and the puritans, of Freud and Menninger.

* * *

The satirist ridicules folly, but respects it; he laughs, lest he weep. The psychoanalyst diagnoses folly and debases it; he weeps, lest he laugh. In short, the former is "hateful" toward those he satirizes, but treats them as equals; whereas the latter is "loving" toward those he analyzes, but treats them as inferiors.

* * *

Cadavers in the Western world are now buried or cremated, leaving no material human remains for birds of prey to feed on. What Western men now leave behind are reputations, and it is on these spiritual remains that the carrions of our modern medical age—the psychoanalysts and psychohistorians—batten.

* * *

Confession is to free association as absolution is to interpretation, as holy water is to cigar smoke, as original sin is to the Oedipus complex, as the soul is to the mental apparatus, as the priest is to the psychoanalyst, as the Vatican is to the Vienna Psychoanalytic Society, as Jesus is to Freud.

* * *

The priest puts the penitent on his knees; the psychoanalyst puts the patient on his back. In each case, the physical arrangement of the encounter symbolizes the dominant theme of the transaction between the participants: the priest wants to make the penitent feel humiliated; the psychoanalyst wants to make the patient feel helpless. Having imposed "original sin" on the penitent and induced "transference neurosis" in the patient, priest and psychoanalyst can proceed to rescue the one from sin and the other from sickness and demand their eternal gratitude for having "saved" them.

*   *   *

Humorless persons make poor patients, and humorless therapists make abominable analysts.

*   *   *

The concept of transference refers, in part, to a certain kind of view of the relationship between analyst and analysand which protects one or both of them from the lure of sexual temptation.

Typically, this is how transference functions as defense. A female patient feels increasingly attracted, personally and sexually, to a male analyst—and, perhaps, vice versa. If the analyst tells the patient that she has a transference to him and he believes this to be true, what this means is that she does not "really" want him sexually (but someone else), which makes it easier for him to control his sexual urges toward the actual person of the client. The concept of transference then functions as a defense for the analyst.

If the client accepts this interpretation, what this means is that she does not "really" want the analyst sexually (but someone else), which makes it easier for her, too, to control her sexual urges toward the actual person of the analyst. The concept of transference then functions as a defense for the analysand.

*   *   *

Analysts doing anaclitic therapy are like Jesuits running an abortion service. The former encourage patients to lean on them, when their ethic demands that they should encourage patients to lean on themselves; the latter would provide a medical intervention when their ethic demands that they eschew it as murder. This is one of the reasons why I consider modern American psychoanalysis, in which analysts do everything but psychoanalysis, a moral obscenity.

* * *

The analyst should be a catalyst, facilitating the patient's confrontation and communication with himself; he should thus mediate between the patient's acknowledged and unacknowledged desires and decisions. In short, the analyst does not change the patient, but helps the patient to change himself. This is one of the reasons why an outsider to the psychoanalytic situation can never know why a patient has not changed as a result of analysis: the analyst might have failed to give the patient the proper kind of help, or the patient might have preferred to remain as he was.

* * *

Psychoanalysts have written millions of words about prostitution, and there is a voluminous psychoanalytic literature on the psychopathology of prostitutes. But, so far as I am aware, psychoanalysts have written not a word about wet-nursing, and there is no psychoanalytic literature on either the mental health or mental illness of wet nurses. And yet what is the difference between these two classes of women? One rents her mammary glands for feeding, the other for fondling; one sells milk, the other milks.

* * *

A dour person may possess many valuable attributes, but

being witty is not one of them; similarly, a psychoanalyst may possess many valuable attributes, but being able to treat illness is not one of them. In short, just as a dour person cannot be witty, so a psychoanalyst cannot be therapeutic. To be sure, a psychoanalyst may help his client, just as a dour person may entertain his friend; but just as there are many kinds of entertainment only some of which qualify as wit, so there are many kinds of help only some of which qualify as treatment.

Mental Illness

Depression: self-accusation and self-pity.

Elation: self-exultation and self-glorification.

Delusion: belief said to be false by someone who does not share it; for example, the Jewish belief that they are the Chosen People is considered to be a delusion by Christians, and the Christian belief that the sacramental wafer is the body of Jesus is considered to be a delusion by Jews.

Delusions of grandeur: metaphorical plea, rejecting pity and requesting envy.

Obsession: persistent, self-administered ideas.

Compulsion: persistent, self-administered commands.

❋ ❋ ❋

Insanity: insubordination—to rules of polite behavior; to parent, husband, or wife; in short, to civilian authority.

Madness: mutiny.

❋ ❋ ❋

The "paranoid" is a person who insists you don't like him, when in fact you don't, but when the polite thing for him to do would be to keep quiet about it.

❋ ❋ ❋

Every human act may be performed in accordance with social expectations or in contravention of them. Many such socially "abnormal" acts are regarded as mental diseases; logically, all such acts could be. The following examples illustrate the logic of classifying socially unconventional behavior—sometimes called the "abuse" of this or that function—as mental illness.

The abuse of the sex act: self-abuse; perversion; rape; homosexuality.

The abuse of eating: anorexia nervosa (self-starvation); obesity; food faddism.

The abuse of drug taking: drug abuse; drug addiction; paranoid schizophrenia (for refusing to take drugs prescribed by physicians).

The abuse of language: hypochondriasis; hysteria; schizophrenia.

The abuse of speech: mutism; catatonia; stuttering.

The abuse of seeing: visual hallucinations; hysterical blindness.

The abuse of hearing: auditory hallucinations; hysterical deafness.

* * *

The immigrant speaks with an accent; the neurotic hears and sees with one. The former imposes his memories on his speech; the latter, on his experiences.

* * *

When a person says that another person is mentally ill, he accuses that person of some wrongdoing; when he says that he is himself mentally ill, he accuses himself of some wrongdoing. In the former case, a person scapegoats another; in the latter, he scapegoats himself.

* * *

What people nowadays call mental illness, especially in a legal context, is not a fact, but a strategy; not a condition, but a policy; in short, it is not a disease that the alleged patient has, but a decision which those who call him mentally ill make about how to act toward him, whether he likes it or not.

* * *

The concept of multiple personality was much in vogue during the turn of the century, when Janet, Kraepelin, and Freud did their pioneering work. This notion illustrates the important role which the imprecise, pseudo-scientific use of language has played in the development of psychiatry. Every person is capable of playing several roles, just as every automobile is capable of running in several gears; to speak of a person having a "multiple personality" thus makes as much sense as speaking of an automobile having a "multiple automobility."

* * *

Psychoanalysis teaches, correctly enough, that neurotic symptoms are due to unresolved, unconscious conflict. However, it would be more accurate to say that neurotic symptoms are due to the fact that the subject (the so-called "neurotic") chooses indecisiveness in the face of conflict: confronted with the necessity of having to choose between two things both of which he wants but only one of which he can have, he refuses to choose, as if hoping that by waiting only a little longer he would be able to have both. In this sense, the neurotic is simply greedy, preferring the pain of his "symptoms" to that of consciously relinquishing something he wants.

* * *

So-called severely mentally ill patients (or "psychotics") often make claims of being the agents or victims of miracles. For example, they say that they are Jesus or that there are snakes in their stomachs, or they articulate the countless similar claims that are said to be the typical

"symptoms" of "schizophrenia." If we regarded such ut-
terances as belonging in a religious rather than in a medical framework, we would deal with those who make
them in a more dignified way: that is, we could declare
our belief in their miraculous powers (to do or to suffer)
and could pay them the homage they thus deserve; or
we could declare our disbelief in their mendacious claims
(to command or to complain) and could sever further
relations with them.

* * *

If mental illness is a defect or handicap which the mentally ill person has and if being mentally ill is like being
black, female, or Jewish—each of these conditions, in
other places and times, having been considered to be de-
fects or handicaps—then the question we might ask is:
Should we treat the mentally ill person as if he or she
were handicapped or as if he or she were not handicapped? "Humanitarians" have maintained that we must
not treat such people as equals, as doing so would be unfair to them; hence we treat them as inferiors, imposing
an inferior status on them—as slaves, women, Jews, madmen—by law. Lovers of liberty have maintained that we
must treat them as equals, as doing anything else would
be unfair not only to them but to everyone else as well;
hence we cannot treat them as either inferiors or
superiors—and cannot impose a special status on them.
In a free society, blacks, women, Jews, and madmen
would thus have to compete freely with whites, men,
Christians, and psychiatrists—and vice versa.

* * *

Ostensibly, the American Psychiatric Association's *Diagnostic and Statistical Manual* is a list of mental diseases;
actually, it is a list of the professions' claims to categories
of conduct. As prospectors stake out claims for mines
which, they suspect, harbor precious minerals, so psychi-

atrists stake out claims for madmen who, they suspect, harbor precious maladies. However, although minerals cannot own mines, madmen—being persons—can own madness. Thus, the only remedy for psychiatric imperialism is to restore madness to its rightful owner, the madman; and to give the psychiatrist access to it only on terms agreeable to the proprietor.

* * *

Whoever "owns" mental illness will presumably take care of it. If the psychiatrists "own" it, they will take care of it; if the psychologists, they will; and if the patients who ostensibly "have" it—then they must take care of it themselves or find someone who will help them to take care of it.

* * *

My suggestion that mental illness is not a disease was immediately and instinctively viewed as an attempt to redistribute the wealth inherent in madness—as if I were proposing taking "mental illnesses" away from the psychiatrists and giving them to the psychologists. Of course, I intended nothing of the sort. Thinking or speaking of so-called mental illnesses as "problems in living" or as "personal problems" does not imply that these phenomena are the property of psychologists. Indeed, I have made it clear from the beginning of my work that the issue of the control or "ownership" of conduct—healthy or sick, sane or insane—is an integral part of the problem of so-called mental illness; that in order to come to grip with these problems we must decide whether we value freedom more than health or vice versa; and that I, placing freedom above health, advocate returning health and illness, mental health and mental illness, to their rightful owners—the so-called patients and mental patients, the persons who "possess" or are said to "possess" these conditions.

* * *

Some of my critics say that I am wrong because what we now call "mental illness" may yet be shown to be, at least in some cases, a type of bodily illness we cannot now so diagnose. But such an advance in the art of diagnosis would only add to the list of conditions we call "diseases"—that is, to the list of literal diseases; it would not impair the validity of my argument that we call some types of behaviors "mental diseases"—and that these are metaphorical diseases.

Others say that I am wrong not because I say that mental illness is unlike bodily illness, an assertion with which they agree; nor because I say that involuntary treatment is not more justified for so-called mental illness than it is for bodily illness, a moral principle with which they also agree; but because the term "mental illness" designates a phenomenologically identifiable category of conduct which they claim is useful for the science of psychology. But, in the first place, these critics are remarkably loath to offer a definition of mental illness—or of mental health; and, in the second place, they seriously underestimate the significance of the principle that, especially in human affairs, the meaning of a word lies in its use. Words such as "crazy," "insane," "mad," "mentally ill," and "psychotic"—have long been used, and continue to be used, to justify involuntary mental hospitalization and treatment.

In short, although it is true that the behaviors of persons who claim to be Jesus or Napoleon differ from those of persons who make no such claims, it is misleading and mischievous merely to describe these differences between them so long as their description justifies the dehumanization and oppression of the former group by the latter.

* * *

Because of the way we now use language, a person is seen as either mentally healthy or mentally ill. When an individual acts in a socially deviant fashion, he or she is called "mentally ill." When I assert that such a person is not mentally ill, it is assumed that I consider him or her to be "mentally healthy." This, of course, is utterly fallacious. Here is why. At the height of the Inquisition, a person was seen as either a faithful Catholic or a heretic. At that time, when an individual acted in a religiously deviant fashion, he or she was called a "heretic." We would now not consider such a person a heretic—but neither would we consider him or her a faithful Catholic. Likewise, it does not follow that by rejecting the concept of mental illness, one commits oneself to the view that those now considered mentally ill are actually mentally healthy. I reject both concepts and terms as false labels for social conformity and deviance.

* * *

To many physicians, loyalty to "scientific medicine" means having blind faith in biological reductionism. They thus believe—or think they ought to believe—that all "mental symptoms," such as obsessions and compulsions, phobias and depressions, and what not, are "nothing but" the expressions of as yet not understood physical and chemical processes in the brain. Were they consistent, they would also believe that the Holy Communion is "nothing but" a snack and that Yom Kippur is "nothing but" a rest for the stomach preliminary to an orgy of gluttony.

* * *

Organic psychiatrists claim that mental diseases are "caused" by or are the "symptoms" of underlying bodily diseases—as yet undiscovered but waiting to be discovered by progress in medical science. If this proved to be true for some or all "mental diseases," it would only add more items to the existing list of "organic diseases" whose treatment patients are free to reject. Hence, evidence supporting the "organic etiology" of so-called mental illness would display rather than dispel the moral and political dilemmas of coercive psychiatry: for if schizophrenia is a disease like multiple sclerosis, why should there be special laws justifying the involuntary diagnosis, confinement, and treatment of schizophrenics but not of multiple sclerotics?

* * *

The mere act of speaking of protecting the "civil rights of mental patients" is an injury to their civil rights. For just as speaking of the "civil rights of slaves" implicitly legitimizes the legal distinction between slaves and free men and hence deprives the former of liberties and dignities enjoyed by the latter, so speaking of the "civil rights of mental patients" implicitly legitimizes the legal distinction between insane patients and sane citizens and hence deprives the former of liberties and dignities enjoyed by the latter.

Not until a free people accept and demand that civil rights be independent of psychiatric criteria, just as they now are of religious criteria and are becoming so with respect to racial and sexual criteria and not until legislators and jurists deprive physicians, and especially psychiatrists, of the power to exercise social controls by means of quasi-medical sanctions will the civil rights of persons accused of mental illness be protected.

* * *

The difference between treating "mental illness" as a role and as a condition is the same as the difference between treating Jewishness as a role and as a condition. It is one thing to ask a person if he is Jewish (and wants to go to the temple); it is another to determine if he is circumcised (and if he is, to send him to a concentration camp). Similarly, it is one thing to ask a person if he is mentally ill (and wants to see a psychiatrist); it is another to determine if he has delusions (and if he does, to send him to a mental hospital).

＊ ＊ ＊

Psychiatrists often claim that mental illnesses have a "biological basis" and act as if proving this would establish that these so-called illnesses are bona-fide diseases. But being a jockey or basketball player also has biological bases—in the conditions of being very short or very tall—but they are nevertheless not diseases.

It is important to keep in mind, then, first, that anything a person does may be said to have a "biological basis," in that he could not do it if he did not have a live body; and, second, that although it makes sense to speak of persons' displaying conditions such as achondroplasia or acromegaly as having diseases, it makes no sense to speak of persons' performing roles such as jockey or basketball player as having diseases.

Myth of Mental Illness

Nearly twenty years ago I suggested that there is, and can be, no such thing as a mental illness. With increasing frequency psychiatrists and psychologists now announce that this or that form of human behavior—for example, schizophrenia or homosexuality or frigidity—is not a symptom or an instance of mental illness. Such claims are attracting much popular attention and support, perhaps because they simultaneously assert and deny the validity of the concept of mental illness: by asserting that X is not a mental illness, they inform about the nature of X and also imply that, although X is not a mental disease, Y and Z are. In short, as formerly people used to want to both believe and disbelieve in the existence of witches, so now they want to both believe and disbelieve in the existence of mental illness.

＊　＊　＊

No sooner had my suggestion that mental illness is not a disease gained a measure of acceptance, than new suggestions were advanced as to what it "really" is. As every conceivable type of human behavior has been labeled mental illness, all of these suggestions are correct, insofar as they identify certain behaviors which are sometimes classified as mental illnesses; and all of them are incorrect, insofar as they imply that these behaviors are "mental" or "illnesses" or that they alone have been called "mental illnesses."

Thus, some persons maintain that mental illness is a form of behavior into which individuals are driven, as it were, by unbearably painful life experiences; others, that it is a form of irresponsible behavior; and still others, that it is a form of socially maladaptive behavior. These are all hopeless attempts to rescue the term "mental illness," doomed to failure by ignoring the fact that emotionally charged terms have lives of their own, not subject to plastic reconstruction by liberal reformers.

*   *   *

Would a psychiatrist give a person a shovel to help him dig for his buried memories? Of course not. But he would give him drugs to relieve him of the pain they cause him. The reason for this difference is that the psychiatrist is the high priest of healing, not of agriculture; that drugs, not shovels, are the sacraments of his ceremonial cures; and that while buried memories are maladies on the psychiatrist's couch, they are metaphors in the farmer's fields.

*   *   *

When we say that someone has "no guts" we mean that he is a coward; we would regard it as absurd to treat him—taking the metaphor literally—with an intestinal transplant.

When we say that someone has a "nervous breakdown" we also mean that he is something like a coward, that he does not accept responsibility for the consequences of his ill-chosen or unlucky actions; but in this case we regard it as eminently reasonable to treat him—taking the metaphor literally—with rest, hospitalization, and drugs, in an effort to "strengthen" his "weak nervous system."

* * *

Calling certain phenomena "mental illnesses" rests on an unwitting misunderstanding or deliberate misuse of language; in particular, on the misunderstanding or misuse of the words by means of which we distinguish actions from movements—for example, designs from diseases.

Consider in this connection what we mean by the word "music." "Music" is the name of certain patterns of sounds which human beings compose, sing, produce with certain kinds of instruments, hear, and enjoy. Yet we also speak of the "music" of leaves rustling in the wind or of waves washing against the shore. Because the latter sounds are pleasing to us and resemble musical sounds, we call them, too, "music"; however, because they are not generated by a human agent, we can—and often do—distinguish them from sounds which are.

The same considerations apply to what we mean by the word "art." Suppose that someone demonstrated, with irrefutable scientific proof and legal evidence, that a certain surrealistic painting, now highly valued as a piece of art, had in fact not been painted by the person to whom its origin is attributed, but had been produced accidentally by a cleaning woman spilling paint on an empty canvas. Would one still want to call it a "painting" or a "work of art"?

I submit that these are our proper models for examining and explaining what we mean by the term "mental illness"; and for what has happened—and will continue to happen—when it is discovered that a person's condition, previously attributed to mental illness, is the consequence of an organic disease of his brain.

We call patterns of paint on canvas "art" only if we believe that they are the results of a human agent's deliberate design; if they are the results of human accident or of nonhuman events, we do not call the resulting objects "paintings" or "art." This is not to say, of course, that such objects may not be esthetically pleasing. Indeed, a piece of driftwood may be much more beautiful than an amateurish wood carving; nevertheless, it would be correct to call the wood carving a "sculpture" or "work of art," but it would be incorrect to so call a piece of driftwood.

Similarly, if the convulsive movements of a person are self-induced—however complicatedly and self-deceptively—we call the phenomenon "hysteria" and consider it, rightly, the paradigm of "mental illness." Whereas if the same sorts of movements are induced by the random firings of certain neurons in the motor cortex, we call the phenomenon "grand mal epilepsy" and no longer consider it an instance of mental illness.

The discovery of the "organic etiology" of any particular mental illness would thus not explain that mental illness more clearly, but would, rather, destroy it as a mental illness—and would replace it with a newly discovered bodily illness. If all mental illnesses were shown to have organic causes, then all of them would be replaced by hitherto unknown bodily illnesses. Were such discoveries to be made, they would represent achievements of the greatest importance; but they would clarify the nature of "mental illness" no more than would the discovery that Shakespeare's works had in fact been written by monkeys typing in the British Museum would clarify the beauty, the meaning, and the values—at once dramatic and moral—of his plays.

* * *

People—especially physicians and medical students—do not understand the fundamental distinction between being sick and being a patient; in other words, that a person may be sick and not be a patient and vice versa. Thus, they fail to see that a Christian Scientist can no more be a patient than a priest can be a husband, or an Orthodox Jew an expert on gourmet cooking, or a Black Muslim a heroin addict. Unable to understand that a person may be a patient and not be sick, they also call such persons "sick," that is, "mentally sick"—which is rather like calling priests "mentally impotent."

The moral: as a good priest is not impotent but abstains from sex, so a good (voluntary, self-defined) mental patient is not sick but abstains from health.

* * *

One of the arguments against my claim that there is no mental illness has hardened into a line which seems to be very effective in impressing people that I am, and must be, wrong. It goes something like this: "We believe in the medical approach to mental illness. There are others [and they may or may not mention me by name] who prefer the social approach. But they are wrong, because . . ."—and then they cite studies about the "genetic determinants" of schizophrenia and the effectiveness of "drugs" controlling this "disease."

I am often confronted with this argument, sometimes by reporters or others from the news media, and have concluded that it is founded on so successful a distortion of my position that it is virtually impossible to counter it. For if a well-meaning questioner does not see the point on which this riddle turns, no amount of fresh explanation about the mythology of mental illness is likely to make him see it. Still, I try to answer it, along this line.

"Let us go back four hundred years. Then people believed in witches, and the official explanation of witchcraft was theological. Now, suppose someone came along and said: 'There are no witches. "Witch" is merely a name that is sometimes attached to poor and helpless people, usually women.' Would it be proper to call this person's position on witches a 'social approach' to witchcraft as against the official 'theological approach' to it? Of course not. What this person offers is not a 'sociological approach' to witches, but a moral and philosophical criticism of the people who call other people 'witches.'"

Since everyone now knows that there are no witches, this explanation satisfies everyone about witchcraft. And since everyone now knows that there are mental diseases, this explanation satisfies no one about psychiatry.

The problem of schizophrenia arises, in part, from the fact that a psychiatrist cannot go into a man's home uninvited and rename his dog; but he can go into his home uninvited and rename him. That is one of the ways in which John Doe becomes a "schizophrenic patient."

*   *   *

It would be stupid to think or say that marriage is something in the head of the wife or husband; actually, it's something—a name, an institution—that holds them together as, and makes them into, wife and husband.

Similarly, it is stupid to think or say that madness (or schizophrenia) is something in the head of the psychotic or the psychiatrist; actually, it's something—a name, an institution—that holds them together as, and makes them into, psychotic patient and psychiatric physician.

*   *   *

The psychiatric matrimony—the relationship between psychotic and psychiatrist, enacted before an audience of relatives, physicians, judges, and other interested onlookers—may be likened to a carefully choreographed dance routine. The psychotic—cast as "patient"—displays the metaphors of dependency, defiance, and disease. The psychiatrist—cast as "doctor"—displays the complementary metaphors of care, control, and cure. Society—cast as the spectators—has grown to love this ballet, has an insatiable appetite for watching it, and demands the periodic staging of new shows. Minor variations in the costumes of the dancers and the choreography of their movements lend freshness to certain new performances, and such innovations are encouraged; but basic changes in the dance routine, or closing down the show, are options which society denies to both the "real patient" and the "real doctor."

*   *   *

Many people called "schizophrenic" are, in effect, persons who want to subjugate others or to be served by them. They make outrageous claims about who they are or what others do to them; write lengthy letters in an illegible handwriting; and so forth. In these and countless other ways they dramatize themselves so as to be perceived by others in one of two ways: as a distressed and helpless child or as a person declaring his refusal to take care of himself and hurling out the challenge: "Now, what are you going to do about *that?*" The "schizophrenic" thus presents an acute, as well as a potentially chronic, problem for his audience, which the latter may try to solve in several ways:

When "schizophrenics" annoy or promise to do so, one may simply avoid or reject them. This is the ordinary, informal sanction people bring to bear against those they don't like: they try to have as little as possible, or nothing, to do with them.

When "schizophrenics" try to seduce one into a relationship with them, one may try to offer to contract with them and then sever the relationship when they break it (which they are likely to do).

When "schizophrenics" break the law, as they often do, they may be dealt with by fines and imprisonment, punishments they may invite and provoke.

When society defines "schizophrenics" as "mentally ill" and "dangerous," they may be dealt with by confinement in mental hospitals, a segregation they may invite and provoke.

What all these alternatives have in common is that they serve to stabilize, for shorter or longer periods, the intolerable human situations—the scandalous "scenes"—in which "schizophrenics" often find themselves, either because they create them or because those they have offended create them.

* * *

"Schizophrenia" is the category—called a "disease"—into which are placed all those who cannot find their place in life, who don't know their place, or whom others want to dislodge from their place.

Those who cannot find their place suffer from, and offend others with, their uncertainties and uselessness. These are the people who used to be diagnosed as suffering from dementia praecox and are diagnosed today as suffering from undifferentiated schizophrenia.

Those who don't know their place offend others by not conforming to social norms: they are either too self-abnegating or too self-aggrandizing, sometimes both, more often the latter. These are the people diagnosed as suffering from simple, hebephrenic, or paranoid schizophrenia.

Finally, there are those whom others want to dislodge from their place because they offend by virtue of their accomplishments, legal or illegal. These are the people who attract attention, as famous criminals or public figures, whom the "ordinary man," acting through the psychiatrist, is only too happy to put in his place—which is that of madman or "schizophrenic."

Thus, because what we call "schizophrenia" is so intimately connected with people knowing and having their proper places in society, it follows logically—and this is consistent with the facts—that the management of schizophrenia revolves centrally around the provision of social spaces for so-called schizophrenics. They used to be incarcerated in insane asylums and madhouses. More recently, they were confined in mental hospitals and psychiatric centers. Now many psychiatrists advocate housing them in a host of new accommodations, ranging from broken-down hotels to the homes of relatives who don't want them. The one conclusion that apparently cannot be seriously entertained is that schizophrenia is, quintessentially, a problem of where the so-called patient should live and how he should support himself; and that, like anyone else not in jail, he should be allowed to live wherever he wants to and can, limited only by his own financial and psychological resources and by those of his community.

* * *

"Hypocrisy," said La Rochefoucauld, "is the homage vice pays to virtue." Just so, schizophrenia is the homage egalitarianism and the classless society pay to the inequality among individuals and to the social stratification which it inexorably generates.

Psychotherapy

Psychotherapy is a myth. Psychotherapeutic interventions are metaphorical treatments that stand in the same sort of relation to medical treatments as criticizing and editing television programs stand to repairing television receivers.

* * *

Psychotherapy is secular ethics: it is the religion of the formally irreligious—with its language, which is not Latin but medical jargon; with its theology, which is not Christianity but positivism; and with its ultimate source of meaning and value, which is not God but science.

* * *

Every method and school of psychotherapy is actually a system of applied ethics couched in the idiom of treatment; and each reflects the personality, values, and aspirations of its founder.

Adler's system is that of a good boy, of an earnest Boy Scout, of an idealistic socialist; the paradigm concept in his system is "social interest."

Freud's system is that of an arrogant adolescent, of a vengeful Jew, of an embittered member of a humiliated class bent—like a would-be Count of Monte Cristo—on a ceaseless campaign of humiliating his former tormentors; the paradigm concept in his system is the "death instinct."

Jung's system is that of a comfortable bourgeois, of a wise clergyman, of a detached student of comparative religion; the paradigm concept in his system is the "collective unconscious."

❊ ❊ ❊

As one man's meat is another man's poison, so one man's psychotherapy is another man's psychopathology.

❊ ❊ ❊

Psychotherapies may be divided into three types or models in accordance with the therapist's attitude toward or expectation from the patient:

1. The indulgent type: "You don't have to give me anything; just get well." 2. The punitive type: "You don't know what you need; I'll take care of you." 3. The contractual type: "You must pay me; and I'll try to help you accomplish what you want."

In the first situation, the patient owes the therapist compliance and gratitude; in the second, self-abasement and submission; in the third, money.

❊ ❊ ❊

Individual psychotherapy is a particular kind of conversation between two people. However, if it were called simply "conversation," one party could not regard himself as ill or deduct his payments for it on his income tax return and the other party could not regard himself as a physician or prevent others from engaging in such conversation.

In short, the medical "blessing" of conversation as "psychotherapy" is like the priestly blessing of water as "holy" or as the rabbinical blessing of pickles as "kosher": each transforms something ordinary into something extraordinary and thus legitimizes those who control it—whether it be something therapeutic, holy, or kosher—in dominating and exploiting the multitudes who want to gain access to it.

* * *

Architects design houses, not homes; homes are what people create, or fail to create, out of their houses.

Similarly, psychotherapists provide conversations, not cures; "cures" (of souls, now called "successful psychotherapies") are what clients who engage in such conversations create, or fail to create, out of their contacts with their psychotherapists.

* * *

What do ideas like "insight" and "self-understanding" refer to? Actually, these terms point to two quite different aspects of self-knowledge: namely, to knowing oneself as object and as agent. In the first instance, a person knows, or has a certain image of, what has happened to him; in the second, he knows, or has a certain image of, what he has done. Psychoanalysis and other "reconstructive" psychotherapies have overemphasized insight of the first type at the expense, or even the exclusion, of insight of the second type. Psychotherapies grounded on the premise that the individual is a moral agent need to redress this imbalance. A person—especially while young and living in his family of origin—is both an object and an agent; his insight—if it is to serve the goal of diminishing his burdens as object and enhancing his powers as agent—must therefore be composed of understanding, equally balanced, of both of these aspects of his self.

* * *

The psychotherapist who calls his conversations with cli-

ents "patient-interviews" and tape records them is like
the traveler who calls strange places and people "tourist
attractions" and "natives" and photographs them. Actually, each puts a mechanical barrier, a gadget, between
himself and his own experience, thus attenuating or
killing it, while at the same time telling himself that he
is trying to preserve it for more perfect future recall. But
by objectifying and recording his experiences, each destroys precisely that which he tries to preserve.

* * *

Typical title for a psychotherapy case presentation at a
medical center: "The treatment of a sixteen-year-old adolescent boy." Since in medicine what is typically treated
is a disease and the title of a typical medical case presentation might be "The treatment of meningococcal
septicemia in a sixteen-year-old boy"—the title of the
psychiatric case presentation reveals that, for psychiatry, being sixteen years old and adolescent is, in itself, a
disease requiring treatment.

* * *

In behavior therapy, insofar as a person is "made" to do
something he is afraid to do and hence does not want to
do, the intervention must be one of two things: coercion
or mock coercion.

If the therapist has real power over the patient—for
example, if the patient is a committed mental patient
and the therapist has legal authority to "treat" him—then
behavior therapy is simply one of the countless ways in
which a person who possesses power controls the conduct of another who does not.

If, on the other hand, the therapist has no real power
over the patient—for example, if the patient is a fee-pay-
ing client in a psychologist's private office—then behavior
therapy is one of the countless ways in which two persons enact scenes of mock coercion, one of the partici-

pants pretending to control, the other pretending to be controlled, and both pretending to believe the other's pretending.

* * *

Authoritarian psychiatrists assert that the aim of psychotherapy is to rid the patient of his anxieties, depressions, and guilts by "making him realize" the irrationality of his symptoms. I say that the aim of psychotherapy should be defined by the patient, not the therapist; that the principal means by which the autonomous psychotherapist can help his client is by listening to him and letting him teach the therapist the rationality of his symptoms; and that only then can the therapist offer his client the additional help of discussing alternative life options and strategies.

* * *

If the psychotherapist or psychoanalyst is a secular-spiritual adviser or guide, as Freud himself had said he was, then we must take to heart the practical implications of that role and its duties. It is not a job like barbering or surgery, making cars or selling shoes. It is, as the Jews of antiquity realized, not a job that can be done full time, year in and year out. The Jews thus expected their rabbis to have "real" jobs, and to be spiritual counselors on the side—not, to be sure, because they considered being a rabbi an unimportant pastime, but, on the contrary, because they understood that it was an activity so laden with moral burdens that it could not form the basis of a regular, daily occupation. Freud, in fact, did not practice psychoanalysis full time; his heart was in his writing. Jung did not practice psychotherapy full time; his heart was in his study of the historical transformation of symbols. Nor, in my opinion, can modern psychiatrists, psychotherapists, and psychoanalysts practice their craft full time—and do justice to their calling.

*   *   *

In Victorian days, mothers who did not want to bother
with feeding their infants hired wet nurses for them.
Today, mothers who do not want to bother talking to
their children and husbands who do not want to bother
talking to their wives hire psychotherapists for them. In
each case, the care of "dependents" is hired out. The
difference is that no one mistook wet nurses, but everyone mistakes psychotherapists, for doctors.

*   *   *

It is impossible to forget something by dint of effort.
Memories, good or bad, cannot be removed as if they
were art objects or useless pieces of junk. Hence, inas-
much as the psychotherapist tries to help his client to
forget, he cannot succeed in this task by approaching his
goal through a direct route; instead, he must help his client understand that the way to forget X is by learning Y,
and the way to achieve superior skill in forgetting (what
one wants to forget) is not by practicing the art of forgetting (since there is no such art), but by practicing the
art of learning.

*   *   *

As there are conflicts among nations in the world, so
there are conflicts among fathers, mothers, and children
in the family. Recommending family therapy for family
conflicts is like recommending the United Nations for
national conflicts. Liberals are fond of both of these
approaches to "conflict resolution." I think both are
harmful, as both conceal conflict and tacitly support, in
the name of "peace" and "mental health," one warring
party against another. In each case, moreover, the strong
has no need for a mediator and will not respect his rec-
ommendations if they are contrary to his self-defined
self-interests; and the weak receives no reliable protection from the mediator against those who aggress against

him and, if he trusts the mediator, is only lulled into a false sense of security by him. In short, as the United Nations helps to finish off the weak nation invaded by the stronger one, so the family therapist helps to finish off the weak family member victimized by the stronger one. This outcome follows inexorably, in the one case, from where the guns come from, and in the other, from where the money comes from.

Science and Scientism

Anthropologist: a person who goes abroad to record and remark on the superstitions of foreigners to conceal those of his own people.

Satirist: anthropologist of his own club, country, and culture; the opposite of anthropologist.

* * *

Primitives treat objects as agents; we call these people "savages" and their outlook on life "animism." Psychiatrists treat agents as objects; we call these people "scientists" and their outlook on life "humanism."

The primitive tries to understand nature in terms of human nature. The psychiatrist tries to understand human nature in terms of nature. Scientists have corrected the savage's mistake. Who will correct the psychiatrist's?

* * *

Animalism is the opposite of humanism. It is treating man as though he were an animal. Science, medicine, and especially psychiatry are often guilty of animalizing man. The theory and practice of conventional psychiatry are, at bottom, the expressions of this tendency. Mental illness is a distinctly human affair. But the more we insist that it is an "illness"—and the more we prove this by producing "experimental neuroses" in animals and by curing human neuroses by means of drugs and shocks and surgery—the more we bestialize, animalize man. Having reduced him to the level of animal, we expect him to act like one—unconcerned about past failures, misdeeds, and wasted opportunities and heedless of the future; in short, unreflective and "happy"—a veritable anti-Socrates.

* * *

In natural science, discoveries are made once by individuals: Einstein discovered relativity, Noguchi the syphilitic origin of paresis. These discoveries were declared to be true because other scientists could quickly verify or confirm them, not because the German Physical Society or the Japanese Medical Society declared them to be true.

In social science, declarations are made twice, by individuals and groups: Mencken said Prohibition was a stupid mistake; I have said that homosexuality is not a mental disease. These declarations were then declared to be true not because anyone verified or confirmed them, but because a constitutional amendment repealed Prohibition and because the American Psychiatric Association struck homosexuality from its official list of mental diseases.

This is another way of saying, and seeing, that while the natural sciences deal with facts and "natural laws," subject to empirical and logical tests—the social sciences deal with judgments and moral or legal laws, subject to personal and popular opinion and political opposition.

* * *

There are fundamental differences between natural and (so-called) social science. In the former, the student must try to understand what "the thing"—for example, oxygen, diabetes, penicillin—*is*, whereas in the latter, he or she must try to understand why the authorities say that "the thing"—for example, crime, schizophrenia, psychoanalysis—is what they *say it is*.

In natural science, in other words, language—conventional and constant—is a tool: it is the microscope revealing a landscape hidden to the naked eye; whereas in social science, language—arbitrary and inconstant—is an impediment: it is the distorting mirror reflecting familiar faces as monstrous masks.

* * *

In natural science, the task is to make new discoveries and to formulate novel theories, and to have the courage of propounding them in opposition to established knowledge; in moral science, it is to rediscover old observations and to rearticulate ancient principles and to have the courage to defend them in opposition to the pretensions of scientism.

* * *

The search for novelty—to see what no one else has seen, to infer what no one else has inferred—occupies a pivotal role in the enterprise which has become known as "natural science." The imitation of this enterprise, in what has become known as "social science," has led not to the identification of new facts, but to the invention of new names for old facts.

The natural scientist is thus a literal scientist: he is an explorer and creator of new facts, relationships, and territories. Whereas the social scientist is a metaphorical scientist: he is an explorer and creator of a new language; he is a poet whose poetry about himself and others is mistaken for prose about "human nature."

* * *

Progress in the science of human behavior now depends on a reversal of interest in the epidemiology and epistemology of mental illness; in other words, it depends on fewer people worrying about the epidemiology and more about the epistemology, say, of schizophrenia.

*   *   *

Today, two of the most important religions are communism and psychiatry. Each is based on the principle, proclaimed by their high priests, that human behavior is determined by scientific laws and that individuals have therefore no free will. And each consists of the practice, zealously pursued by their leading practitioners, of systematically depriving individuals of the freedom to make uncoerced choices.

Therapeutic State

In a capitalist society a person can—or ought to be able to—obtain narcotics (such as opium, morphine, codeine, etc.) in exchange for money. In a therapeutic society, a person can—and ought to be able to—obtain narcotics only in exchange for pain.

The former social policy encourages some people to divert their economic resources to satisfying their desires; the latter encourages them to divert their existential resources to satisfying their desires. In short, as capitalism generates purchasers and producers of goods and services, so therapeutism generates patients and doctors, addicts and pushers.

* * *

One of the favorite slogans of the modern, "enlightened" physician is: "There is no point in just treating rat bites and ignoring the rats." When rat bites man, the obvious thing to do is to control the rats. These physicians and their "liberal" followers then plunge ahead and conclude that when man bites himself, the obvious thing to do is to pull out his teeth or to muzzle him. They thus maintain that when people get, say, lung cancer from smoking, there is no point in just treating the cancer and ignoring the smoking. Such a single-minded pursuit of health begins with the control of rats, and ends with the control of men.

*   *   *

A familiar adage about education declares: "Those who can, do; those who can't, teach." This may now be adapted to medicine or the so-called "delivery of health care": "Those who can, practice; those who can't, plan."

*   *   *

The FDA calls certain substances "controlled." But there are no "controlled substances," there are only controlled citizens.

*   *   *

Missionary clerics define natives as "heathen," the better to be able to save them. Missionary clinicians define people as "patients," the better to be able to cure them.

*   *   *

The most important characteristic of the last three centuries of human history is often said to be the decline of religion and the development of science. Only the second half of this view is true: science and technology have made gigantic advances during this period; religion, however, has undergone a profound change, rather than a major decline. This religious metamorphosis consists of the magicalization of science, yielding scientism, and of the medicalization of (the Christian) religion, yielding psychiatry and (compulsory) therapy.

*   *   *

As rule by God through priests is called "theocracy," so rule by Medicine through physicians should be called "pharmacracy." Accordingly, the Department of Health, Education and Welfare and the National Institutes of Health and What-not are the American Medical Vatican;

state health departments are the bishoprics; hospitals are the cathedrals; drugs are the holy sacraments; and physicians are the priests and patients the penitents of our American Medical Church.

* * *

When ceremonial religion ruled, only priests could hear confessions; when it ceased to rule, it lost its power to appoint confessors and impose them on the people. Since then, the people could hire their own confessors (and could call them anything from "pastors" to "psychotherapists").

Similarly, when ceremonial medicine rules, only physicians can dispense (dangerous) drugs; when it will cease to rule, it will lose its power to appoint drug experts and impose them on the people. Then, the people will be able to hire their own drug experts (and call them anything from "pharmacologists" to "pharmacomythologists").

* * *

When Marie Antoinette was told that the poor people of France had no bread, she is said to have remarked: "Let them eat cake." That, of course, was in the good old days, when people provided, as best they could, for their own basic needs. Today, when the state often provides these for them, it does not merely *let* poor people eat cake—it *makes* them eat it! Here is a typical example.

In a Manhattan "welfare hotel" where there are approximately ten arrests per month for crimes ranging from burglary to rape and attempted murder and where the tenants are furnished little or no heat and are afraid to leave their apartments lest they be broken into while they are away, an association of the tenants petitions for improvements. This is what they get: "Mr. Lebowitz [the president of the block association] said that the management . . . had sometimes been co-operative in seeking improvements, such as allowing Roosevelt Hospital to open a community psychiatric treatment unit in the building. . . ."*

In short, when Frenchmen wanted bread but were too poor to buy it, they were told to eat cake; when Americans want policemen to protect their safety, they are given psychiatrists to protect their mental health.

* * *

In Welfare and Therapeutic States, human and medical services are free, but people are not; in open societies, people are free, but nothing else is.

* * *

In a free society everything that is not prohibited is permitted; this is the right to liberty.

In a totalitarian society, everything that is not permitted is prohibited; this is the right to obedience.

In a therapeutic society, everything that is not prohibited is required; that is the right to treatment.

* * *

The basic premise of the Theological State is that there is a God; that He has created everything, including the human body and its diseases; and that people may therefore not tamper with what belongs to God. Hence the passivist, priestly attitude toward disease, as exemplified by the prohibition against the dissection of dead bodies.

The basic premise of the Therapeutic State is that there is no God; that the human body belongs to the state or the medical profession (or to some combination of them); and that—in the name of "treatment," approved by physicians and politicians—people may therefore do anything to it. Hence the activist medical attitude toward disease, as exemplified by the state-mandated

---

* New York *Times*, Nov. 27, 1972, p. 39.

removal of body parts from healthy children for transplantation into the bodies of their siblings.

* * *

By prescribing literal treatments for diseases and metaphorical treatments for disagreements and by assuming the power to impose such treatments on those who do not submit to them voluntarily, the Therapeutic State aspires to become one of the most hideous tyrannies in human history.

Epilogue

"The world is kept alive only by heretics. . . . Our symbol of faith is heresy: tomorrow is inevitably heresy to today. . . . Yesterday, there was a tsar, and there were slaves; today there is no tsar, but the slaves remain; tomorrow there will be only tsars. We march in the name of tomorrow's free man—the royal man. We have lived through the epoch of suppression of the masses; we are living in an epoch of suppression of the individual in the name of the masses; tomorrow will bring the liberation of the individual—in the name of man. . . . The only weapon worthy of man—of tomorrow's man—is the word."

Yevgeny Zamyatin (1884–1937)*

* Y. Zamyatin, "Tomorrow [1919–20]," in *A Soviet Heretic: Essays by Yevgeny Zamyatin*, edited and translated by Mirra Ginsburg (Chicago: University of Chicago Press, 1970), pp. 51–52.